Great Speeches by American Women

DOVER · THRIFT · EDITIONS

Great Speeches by American Women

Edited by
James Daley

DOVER PUBLICATIONS, INC.
Mineola, New York

DOVER THRIFT EDITIONS

GENERAL EDITOR: MARY CAROLYN WALDREP
EDITOR OF THIS VOLUME: SUSAN L. RATTINER

ACKNOWLEDGMENTS: See page xi.

Bibliographical Note

This Dover edition, first published in 2008, is a new anthology of twenty-one speeches reprinted from standard texts. A new Introduction and Notes to the speakers have been specially prepared for the present edition by James Daley.

Library of Congress Cataloging-in-Publication Data

Great speeches by American women / edited by James Daley.
     p. cm. — (Dover thrift editions)
   ISBN-13: 978-0-486-46141-0
   ISBN-10: 0-486-46141-6
   1. Speeches, addresses, etc., American—Women authors. I. Daley, James,
1979–

PS663.W65G74 2008
815.008'09287—dc22

2007026700

Manufactured in the United States of America
Dover Publications, Inc., 31 East 2nd Street, Mineola, N.Y. 11501

Note

On July 19, 1848, over three hundred women, and forty men, arrived at Wesleyan Chapel in Seneca Falls, New York, to attend the United States of America's first ever women's rights convention. Organized by prominent civil rights advocates Elizabeth Cady Stanton and Lucretia Mott, the Seneca Falls Convention would come to be known as the "birthplace of feminism" in no small part due to the signing of Stanton's visionary document, the "Declaration of Sentiments." Modeled after the Declaration of Independence, this new document was rife with Jeffersonian language, demanding, among other things, women's suffrage, equality in marriage, equality of employment, and equal rights to property for men and women alike.

With the Seneca Falls Convention, a new era in our nation's history was born, even though it would be several decades before many of its founder's demands were met. Throughout this time, however, the history of women's contributions to this nation has not been limited to the struggle for women's rights alone. Our nation owes whatever prosperity, enlightenment, and success it has achieved to the hard work and dedication of the millions upon millions of women who have given their lives and their efforts to its service.

Thus, it was not solely with an eye towards the history of women's rights and feminism that the present anthology has been compiled; rather, the selection contained herein seeks to find examples in all areas of public life where women have played a valued part in shaping this country into what it is today. Although there is still more work to be done to achieve true equality, today America's young women stand to inherit a nation where they are heir to more opportunity than any generation before them. Speaking for two centuries of American women upon her election as Speaker of the House, Nancy Pelosi puts it this way:

> Never losing faith, we waited through the many years of struggle to achieve our rights. But women weren't just waiting; women were working. Never losing faith, we worked to redeem the promise of America, that all men and women are created equal. For our daughters and granddaughters, today we have broken the marble ceiling. For our daughters and our granddaughters, the sky is the limit, anything is possible for them.

JAMES DALEY
Editor

Contents

Acknowledgments

"A Century of Progress of Negro Women" by Mary McLeod Bethune, reprinted with the permission of the Mary McLeod Bethune Foundation, Bethune Cookman College, Daytona Beach, Florida.

"Vice Presidential Nomination Acceptance Address" by Geraldine Ferraro, reprinted with the permission of Geraldine Ferraro.

"Democratic National Convention Keynote Address" by Ann Richards, reprinted with the permission of the Ann Richards Papers, Center for American History, University of Texas at Austin.

"A Whisper of AIDS" by Mary Fisher, reprinted with the permission of the Mary Fisher Clinical AIDS Research and Education (CARE) Fund.

"A 21st Century Feminism" by Gloria Steinem, reprinted with the permission of Gloria Steinem.

"The New Feminism" by Jane Fonda, reprinted with the permission of Jane Fonda.

Sojourner Truth

(1797–1883)

AIN'T I A WOMAN?
May 29, 1851

Sojourner Truth, born Isabella Baumfree, was a slave in Ulster County, New York, until gaining her freedom in 1827. In 1843 she took the name Sojourner Truth and began her lauded career as an abolitionist and feminist. The following speech was given by Truth at a women's rights convention in Akron, Ohio. It was offered largely in response to a clergyman who had previously argued that women were too weak and helpless to be given the right to vote.

WELL, CHILDREN, where there is so much racket there must be something out of kilter. I think that 'twixt the Negroes of the South and the women at the North, all talking about rights, the white men will be in a fix pretty soon. But what's all this here talking about?

That man over there says that women need to be helped into carriages, and lifted over ditches, and to have the best place everywhere. Nobody ever helps me into carriages, or over mud-puddles, or gives me any best place! And ain't I a woman? Look at me! Look at my arm! I have ploughed and planted, and gathered into barns, and no man could head me! And ain't I a woman? I could work as much and eat as much as a man—when I could get it—and bear the lash as well! And ain't I a woman? I have borne thirteen children, and seen most all sold off to slavery, and when I cried out with my mother's grief, none but Jesus heard me! And ain't I a woman?

Then they talk about this thing in the head; what's this they call it? [member of audience whispers, "intellect"] That's it, honey. What's that got to do with women's rights or Negroes' rights? If my cup won't hold but a pint, and yours holds a quart, wouldn't you be mean not to let me have my little half measure full?

Then that little man in black there, he says women can't have as much rights as men, 'cause Christ wasn't a woman! Where did your Christ come from? Where did your Christ come from? From God and a woman! Man had nothing to do with Him.

If the first woman God ever made was strong enough to turn the world upside down all alone, these women together ought to be able to turn it back, and get it right side up again! And now they is asking to do it, the men better let them.

Obliged to you for hearing me, and now old Sojourner ain't got nothing more to say.

Lucretia Mott

(1793–1880)

WHY SHOULD NOT WOMAN SEEK TO BE A REFORMER?
October 18, 1854

*Lucretia Coffin Mott was an active figure in the nineteenth-century re-
form movements, but was best known for her work as an abolitionist and
suffragette. Along with Elizabeth Cady Stanton, Mott initiated the
Seneca Falls Women's Rights Convention in 1848, and in 1850
published "Discourse on Women," her famous treatise on the societal
restrictions on women in Western Europe and America. The following
speech was delivered at the 5th National Women's Rights Convention
in Philadelphia on October 18, 1854.*

I HAVE NOT come here with a view of answering any particular parts
of the lecture alluded to, in order to point out the fallacy of its reasoning. The speaker, however, did not profess to offer anything like argument on that occasion, but rather a sentiment. I have no prepared
address to deliver to you, being unaccustomed to speak in that way;
but I felt a wish to offer some views for your consideration, though
in a desultory manner, which may lead to such reflection and discussion as will present the subject in a true light.

Why should not woman seek to be a reformer? If she is to shrink
from being such an iconoclast as shall "break the image of man's
lower worship," as so long held up to view; if she is to fear to exercise
her reason, and her noblest powers, lest she should be thought to "attempt to act the man," and not "acknowledge his supremacy"; if she
is to be satisfied with the narrow sphere assigned her by man, nor
aspire to a higher, lest she should transcend the bounds of female
delicacy; truly it is a mournful prospect for woman. We would admit
all the difference, that our great and beneficent Creator has made, in

the relation of man and woman, nor would we seek to disturb this relation; but we deny that the present position of woman is her true sphere of usefulness; nor will she attain to this sphere, until the disabilities and disadvantages, religious, civil, and social, which impede her progress, are removed out of her way. These restrictions have enervated her mind and paralyzed her powers. While man assumes that the present is the original state designed for woman, that the existing "differences are not arbitrary nor the result of accident," but grounded in nature; she will not make the necessary effort to obtain her just rights, lest it should subject her to the kind of scorn and contemptuous manner in which she has been spoken of.

So far from her "ambition leading her to attempt to act the man," she needs all the encouragement she can receive, by the removal of obstacles from her path, in order that she may become the "true woman." As it is desirable that man should act a manly and generous part, not "mannish," so let woman be urged to exercise a dignified and womanly bearing, not womanish. Let her cultivate all the graces and proper accomplishments of her sex, but let not these degenerate into a kind of effeminacy, in which she is satisfied to be the mere plaything or toy of society, content with her outward adornings, and the flattery and fulsome adulation too often addressed to her.

Did Elizabeth Fry lose any of her feminine qualities by the public walk into which she was called? Having performed the duties of a mother to a large family, feeling that she owed a labor of love to the poor prisoner, she was empowered by Him who sent her forth, to go to kings and crowned heads of the earth, and ask audience of these, and it was granted her. Did she lose the delicacy of woman by her acts? No. Her retiring modesty was characteristic of her to the latest period of her life. It was my privilege to enjoy her society some years ago, and I found all that belonged to the feminine in woman—to true nobility, in a refined and purified moral nature. Is Dorothea Dix throwing off her womanly nature and appearance in the course she is pursuing? In finding duties abroad, has any "refined man felt that something of beauty has gone forth from her"? To use the contemptuous word applied in the lecture alluded to, is she becoming "mannish"? Is she compromising her womanly dignity in going forth to seek to better the condition of the insane and afflicted? Is not a beautiful mind and a retiring modesty still conspicuous in her?

Indeed, I would ask, if this modesty is not attractive also, when manifested in the other sex? It was strikingly marked in Horace Mann, when presiding over the late National Educational Convention in this city. The retiring modesty of William Ellery Channing was beautiful, as well as of many others who have filled elevated stations in society. These virtues, differing as they may in degree in man and woman, are of the same nature, and call forth our admiration wherever manifested.

The noble courage of Grace Darling is justly honored for risking her own life on the coast of England, during the raging storm, in order to rescue the poor, suffering, shipwrecked mariner.

Woman was not wanting in courage in the early ages. In war and bloodshed this trait was often displayed. Grecian and Roman history have lauded and honored her in this character. English history records her courageous women too, for unhappily we have little but the records of war handed down to us. The courage of Joan of Arc was made the subject of a popular lecture not long ago by one of our intelligent citizens. But more noble, moral daring is marking the female character at the present time, and better worthy of imitation. As these characteristics come to be appreciated in man too, his warlike acts with all the miseries and horrors of the battleground will sink into their merited oblivion, or be remembered only to be condemned. The heroism displayed in the tented field must yield to the moral and Christian heroism which is shadowed in the signs of our times.

The lecturer regarded the announcement of woman's achievements, and the offering of appropriate praise through the press, as a gross innovation upon the obscurity of female life—he complained that the exhibition of attainments of girls in schools was now equal to that of boys, and the newspapers announce that "Miss Brown received the first prize for English grammar," etc. If he objected to so much excitement of emulation in schools, it would be well; for the most enlightened teachers discountenance these appeals to love of approbation and self-esteem. But while prizes continue to be awarded, can any good reason be given why the name of the girl should not be published as well as that of the boy? He spoke with scorn, that "we hear of Mrs. President so and so; and committees and secretaries of the same sex." But if women can conduct their own business, by means of presidents and secretaries of their own sex, can he tell us why they should not? They will never make much progress in any moral movement while they depend upon men to act for them. Do we shrink from reading the announcement that Mrs. Somerville is made an honorary member of a scientific association? That Miss Herschel has made some discoveries, and is prepared to take her equal part in science? Or that Miss Mitchell, of Nantucket, has lately discovered a planet, long looked for? I cannot conceive why "honor to whom honor is due" should not be rendered to woman as well as man; nor will it necessarily exalt her, or foster feminine pride. This propensity is found alike in male and female, and it should not be ministered to improperly in either sex.

In treating upon the affections, the lecturer held out the idea that as manifested in the sexes they were opposite if not somewhat antagonistic, and required a union as in chemistry to form a perfect whole. The simile appeared to me far from a correct illustration of the true union. Minds that can assimilate, spirits that are congenial, attract one another. It is the union of similar, not of opposite affections, which is necessary for the perfection of the marriage bond. There seemed a want of proper delicacy in his representing man as being bold in the demonstration of the pure affection of love. In persons of refinement, true love seeks concealment in man as well as in woman. I will not enlarge upon the subject, although it formed so great a part of his lecture. The contrast drawn seemed a fallacy, as has much, very much, that has been presented in the sickly sentimental strains of the poet from age to age.

The question is often asked, "What does woman want, more than she enjoys? What is she seeking to obtain? Of what rights is she deprived? What privileges are withheld from her?" I answer, she asks nothing as favor, but as right; she wants to be acknowledged a moral, responsible being. She is seeking not to be governed by laws in the making of which she has no voice. She is deprived of almost every right in civil society, and is a cipher in the nation, except in the right of presenting a petition. In religious society her disabilities have greatly retarded her progress. Her exclusion from the pulpit or ministry, her duties marked out for her by her equal brother man, subject to creeds, rules, and disciplines made for her by him, is unworthy her true dignity.

In marriage there is assumed superiority on the part of the husband, and admitted inferiority with a promise of obedience on the part of the wife. This subject calls loudly for examination in order that the wrong may be redressed. Customs suited to darker ages in Eastern countries are not binding upon enlightened society. The solemn covenant of marriage may be entered into without these lordly assumptions and humiliating concessions and promises.

There are large Christian denominations who do not recognize such degrading relations of husband and wife. They ask no aid from magistrate or clergyman to legalize or sanctify this union. But acknowledging themselves in the presence of the Highest and invoking His assistance, they come under reciprocal obligations of fidelity and affection, before suitable witnesses. Experience and observation go to prove that there may be as much harmony, to say the least, in such a union, and as great purity and permanence of affection, as can exist where the common ceremony is observed.

The distinctive relations of husband and wife, of father and mother of a family, are sacredly preserved, without the assumption of authority on the one part, or the promise of obedience on the other. There is nothing in such a marriage degrading to woman. She does not compromise her dignity or self-respect; but enters married life upon equal ground, by the side of her husband. By proper education, she understands her duties, physical, intellectual, and moral; and fulfilling these, she is a helpmeet in the true sense of the word.

I tread upon delicate ground in alluding to the institutions of religious associations; but the subject is of so much importance that all which relates to the position of woman should be examined apart from the undue veneration which ancient usage receives.

> "Such dupes are men to custom, and so prone
> To reverence what is ancient, and can plead
> A course of long observance for its use,
> That even servitude, the worst of ills,
> Because delivered down from sire to son,
> Is kept and guarded as a sacred thing."

So with woman. She has so long been subject to the disabilities and restrictions with which her progress has been embarrassed, that she has become enervated, her mind to some extent paralyzed; and like those still more degraded by personal bondage, she hugs her chains. Liberty is often presented in its true light, but it is liberty for man. I would not go so far, either as regards the abject slave or woman; for in both cases they may be so degraded by the crushing influences around them, that they may not be sensible of the blessings of freedom. Liberty is not less a blessing, because oppression has so long darkened the mind that it can not appreciate it. I would, therefore, urge that woman be placed in such a situation in society, by the recognition of her rights, and have such opportunities for growth and development, as shall raise her from this low, enervated, and paralyzed condition, to a full appreciation of the blessing of entire freedom of mind.

It is with reluctance that I make the demand for the political rights of women, because this claim is so distasteful to the age. Woman shrinks, in the present state of society, from taking any interest in politics. The events of the French Revolution, and the claim for woman's rights, are held up to her as a warning. Let us not look at the excesses of women alone, at that period; but remember that the age was marked with extravagances and wickedness in men as well as women. Political life abounds with these excesses and with shameful outrage. Who knows but that if woman acted her part in governmental affairs, there might be an entire change in the turmoil of political life? It becomes man to speak modestly of his ability to act without her. If woman's judgment were exercised, why might she not aid in making the laws by which she is governed? Lord Brougham remarked that the works of Harriet Martineau upon Political Economy were not excelled by those of any political writer of the present time. The first few chapters of her "Society in America," her views of a Republic, and of government generally, furnish evidence of woman's capacity to embrace subjects of universal interest.

Far be it from me to encourage women to vote, or to take an active part in politics in the present state of our government. Her right to the elective franchise, however, is the same, and should be yielded to her, whether she exercise that right or not. Would that man, too, would have no participation in a government recognizing the life-taking principle; retaliation and the sword. It is unworthy a Christian nation. But when in the diffusion of light and intelligence a Convention shall be called to make regulations for self-government on Christian principles, I can see no good reason why women should not participate in such an assemblage, taking part equally with man.

Professor Walker, of Cincinnati, in his "Introduction to American Law," says: "With regard to political rights, females form a positive exception to the general doctrine of equality. They have no part or lot in the formation or administration of government. They cannot vote or hold office. We require them to contribute their share in the way of taxes to the support of government, but allow them no voice in its direction. We hold them amenable to the laws when made, but allow them no share in making them. This language applied to males would be the exact definition of political slavery; applied to females custom does not teach us so to regard it." Woman, however, is beginning so to regard it.

He further says: "The law of husband and wife, as you gather it from the books, is a disgrace to any civilized nation. The theory of the law degrades the wife almost to the level of slaves. When a woman marries, we call her condition coverture, and speak of her as a *femme covert*. The old writers call the husband baron, and sometimes in plain English, lord. . . . The merging of her name in that of her husband is emblematic of the fate of all her legal rights. The torch of Hymen serves but to light the pile on which these rights are offered up. The legal theory is, that marriage makes the husband and wife one person, and that person is the husband. On this subject, reform is loudly called for. There is no foundation in reason or expediency for the absolute and slavish subjection of the wife to the husband, which forms the foundation of the present legal relations. Were woman, in point of fact, the abject thing which the law in theory considers her to be when married, she would not be worthy the companionship of man."

I would ask if such a code of laws does not require change? If such a condition of the wife in society does not claim redress? On no good ground can reform be delayed. Blackstone says: "The very being and legal existence of woman is suspended during marriage; incorporated or consolidated into that of her husband under whose protection and cover she performs everything." Hurlbut, in his Essay upon Human Rights, says: "The laws touching the rights of women are at variance with the laws of the Creator. Rights are human rights, and pertain to human beings without distinction of sex. Laws should not be made for man or for woman, but for mankind. Man was not born to command, nor woman to obey. . . . The law of France, Spain, and Holland, and one of our own States, Louisiana, recognizes the wife's right to property, more than the common law of England. . . . The laws depriving woman of the right of property are handed down to us from dark and feudal times, and are not consistent with the wiser, better, purer spirit of the age. The wife is a mere pensioner on the bounty of her husband. Her lost rights are appropriated to himself. But justice and benevolence are abroad in our land awakening the spirit of inquiry and innovation; and the Gothic fabric of the British law will fall before it, save where it is based upon the foundation of truth and justice."

May these statements lead you to reflect upon this subject, that you may know what woman's condition is in society, what her restrictions are, and seek to remove them. In how many cases in our country the husband and wife begin life together, and by equal industry and united effort accumulate to themselves a comfortable home. In the event of the death of the wife the household remains undisturbed, his farm or his workshop is not broken up or in any way molested. But when the husband dies he either gives his wife a portion of their joint accumulation, or the law apportions to her a share; the homestead is broken up, and she is dispossessed of that which she earned equally with him; for what she lacked in physical strength she made up in constancy of labor and toil, day and evening. The sons then coming into possession of the property, as has been the custom until of later time, speak of having to keep their mother, when she in reality is aiding to keep them. Where is the justice of this state of things? The change in the law of this State and of New York in relation to the property of the wife, goes to a limited extent toward the redress of these wrongs which are far more extensive and involve much more than I have time this evening to point out.

On no good ground can the legal existence of the wife be suspended during marriage, and her property surrendered to her husband. In the intelligent ranks of society the wife may not in point of fact be so degraded as the law would degrade her; because public sentiment is above the law. Still, while the law stands, she is liable to the disabilities which it imposes. Among the ignorant classes of society, woman is made to bear heavy burdens, and is degraded almost to the level of the slave. There are many instances now in our city, where the wife suffers much from the power of the husband to claim all that she can earn with her own hands. In my intercourse with the poorer class of people, I have known cases of extreme cruelty from the hard earnings of the wife being thus robbed by the husband, and no redress at law.

An article in one of the daily papers lately presented the condition of needle-women in England. There might be a presentation of this class in our own country which would make the heart bleed. Public attention should be turned to this subject in order that avenues of more profitable employment may be opened to women. There are many kinds of business which women, equally with men, may follow with respectability and success. Their talents and energies should be called forth, and their powers brought into the highest exercise. The efforts of women in France are sometimes pointed to in ridicule and sarcasm, but depend upon it, the opening of profitable employment to women in that country is doing much for the enfranchisement of the sex. In England and America it is not an uncommon thing for a wife to take up the business of her deceased husband and carry it on with success.

Our respected British Consul stated to me a circumstance which occurred some years ago, of an editor of a political paper having died in England; it was proposed to his wife, an able writer, to take the editorial chair. She accepted. The patronage of the paper was greatly increased, and she a short time since retired from her labors with a handsome fortune. In that country, however, the opportunities are by no means general for woman's elevation.

In visiting the public school in London a few years since, I noticed that the boys were employed in linear drawing, and instructed upon the black-board in the higher branches of arithmetic and mathematics; while the girls, after a short exercise in the mere elements of arithmetic, were seated during the bright hours of the morning, stitching wristbands. I asked why there should be this difference made; why the girls too should not have the black-board? The answer was, that they would not probably fill any station in society requiring such knowledge.

The demand for a more extended education will not cease until girls and boys have equal instruction in all the departments of useful knowledge. We have as yet no high-school in this State. The normal school may be a preparation for such an establishment. In the late convention for general education, it was cheering to hear the testimony borne to woman's capabilities for head teachers of the public schools. A resolution there offered for equal salaries to male and female teachers when equally qualified, as practiced in Louisiana, I regret to say, was checked in its passage by Bishop Potter; by him who has done so much for the encouragement of education, and who gave his countenance and influence to that Convention. Still, the fact of such a resolution being offered, augurs a time coming for woman which she may well hail. At the last examination of the public schools in this city, one of the alumni delivered an address on Woman, not as is too common in eulogistic strains, but directing the attention to the injustice done to woman in her position in society in a variety of ways, the unequal wages she receives for her constant toil, etc., presenting facts calculated to arouse attention to the subject.

Women's property has been taxed equally with that of men's to sustain colleges endowed by the States; but they have not been permitted to enter those high seminaries of learning. Within a few years, however, some colleges have been instituted where young women are admitted upon nearly equal terms with young men; and numbers are availing themselves of their long denied rights. This is among the signs of the times, indicative of an advance for women. The book of knowledge is not opened to her in vain. Already is she aiming to occupy important posts of honor and profit in our country. We have three females editors in our State and some in other States of the Union. Numbers are entering the medical profession; one received a diploma last year; others are preparing for a like result.

Let woman then go on, not asking favors, but claiming as right, the removal of all hindrances to her elevation in the scale of being; let her receive encouragement for the proper cultivation of all her powers, so that she may enter profitably into the active business of life; employing her own hands in ministering to her necessities, strengthening her physical being by proper exercise and observance of the laws of health. Let her not be ambitious to display a fair hand and to promenade the fashionable streets of our city, but rather, coveting earnestly the best gifts, let her strive to occupy such walks in society as will befit her true dignity in all the relations of life. No fear that she will then transcend the proper limits of female delicacy. True modesty will be as fully preserved in acting out those important vocations, as in the nursery or at the fireside ministering to man's self-indulgence. Then in the marriage union, the independence of the husband and wife will be equal, their dependence mutual, and their obligations reciprocal.

In conclusion, let me say, with Nathaniel P. Willis: "Credit not the old-fashioned absurdity that woman's is a secondary lot, ministering to the necessities of her lord and master! It is a higher destiny I would award you. If your immortality is as complete, and your gift of mind as capable as ours of increase and elevation, I would put no wisdom of mine against God's evident allotment. I would charge you to water the undying bud, and give it healthy culture, and open its beauty to the sun; and then you may hope that when your life is bound up with another, you will go on equally and in a fellowship that shall pervade every earthly interest."

Susan B. Anthony

(1820–1906)

ON BEHALF OF THE WOMAN SUFFRAGE AMENDMENT
January 23, 1880

Susan Brownell Anthony was one of the most prominent and well-known civil rights leaders of the nineteenth century. Remembered mostly as an outspoken crusader for women's suffrage, Susan B. Anthony was also an important abolitionist and a pioneering figure in the temperance movement. The following address, delivered before the Committee on the Judiciary in the U.S. Senate in 1880, is a passionate appeal for the adoption of a women's suffrage amendment.

MR. CHAIRMAN AND GENTLEMEN: Mrs. Spencer said that I would make an argument. I do not propose to do so, because I take it for granted that the members of this committee understand that we have all the argument on our side, and such an argument would be simply a series of platitudes and maxims of government. The theory of this Government from the beginning has been perfect equality to all the people. That is shown by every one of the fundamental principles, which I need not stop to repeat. Such being the theory, the application would be, of course, that all persons not having forfeited their right to representation in the Government should be possessed of it at the age of twenty-one. But instead of adopting a practice in conformity with the theory of our Government, we began first by saying that all men of property were the people of the nation upon whom the Constitution conferred equality of rights. The next step was that all white men were the people to whom should be practically applied the fundamental theories. There we halt to-day and stand at a deadlock, so far as the application of our theory may go. We women have been standing before the American republic for thirty years, asking the men to take yet one step further and extend the practical applica-

13

tion of the theory of equality of rights to all the people to the other half of the people—the women. That is all that I stand here to-day to attempt to demand.

Of course, I take it for granted that the committee are in sympathy at least with the reports of the Judiciary Committees presented both in the Senate and the House. I remember that after the adoption of the fourteenth and fifteenth amendments Senator Edmunds reported on the petition of the ten thousand foreign-born citizens of Rhode Island who were denied equality of rights in Rhode Island simply because of their foreign birth; and in that report held that the amendments were enacted and attached to the Constitution simply for men of color, and therefore that their provisions could not be so construed as to bring within their purview the men of foreign birth in Rhode Island. Then the House Committee on the Judiciary, with Judge Bingham, of Ohio, at its head, made a similar report upon our petitions, holding that because those amendments were made essentially with the black men in view, therefore their provisions could not be extended to the women citizens of this country or to any class except men citizens of color.

I voted in the State of New York in 1872 under the construction of those amendments, which we felt to be the true one, that all persons born in the United States, or any State thereof, and under the jurisdiction of the United States, were citizens, and entitled to equality of rights, and that no State could deprive them of their equality of rights. I found three young men, inspectors of election, who were simple enough to read the Constitution and understand it in accordance with what was the letter and what should have been its spirit. Then, as you will remember, I was prosecuted by the officers of the Federal court, and the cause was carried through the different courts in the State of New York, in the northern district, and at last I was brought to trial at Canandaigua.

When Mr. Justice Hunt was brought from the supreme bench to sit upon that trial, he wrested my case from the hands of the jury altogether, after having listened three days to testimony, and brought in a verdict himself of guilty, denying to my counsel even the poor privilege of having the jury polled. Through all that trial when I, as a citizen of the United States, as a citizen of the State of New York and city of Rochester, as a person who had done something at least that might have entitled her to a voice in speaking for herself and for her class, in all that trial I not only was denied my right to testify as to whether I voted or not, but there was not one single woman's voice to be heard nor to be considered, except as witnesses, save when it came to the judge asking, "Has the prisoner anything to say why sentence shall not be pronounced?" Neither as judge, nor as attorney, nor as jury was I allowed any person who could be legitimately called my peer to speak for me.

Then, as you will remember, Mr. Justice Hunt not only pronounced the verdict of guilty, but a sentence of $100 fine and costs of prosecution. I said to him, "May it please your honor, I do not propose to pay it;" and I never have paid it, and I never shall. I asked your honorable bodies of Congress the next year—in 1874—to pass a resolution to remit that fine. Both Houses refused it; the committees reported against it; though through Benjamin F. Butler, in the House, and a member of your committee, and Matthew H. Carpenter, in the Senate, there were plenty of precedents brought forward to show that in cases of multitudes of men fines had been remitted. I state this merely to show the need of woman to speak for herself, to be as judge, to be as juror.

Mr. Justice Hunt in his opinion stated that suffrage was a fundamental right, and therefore a right that belonged to the State. It seemed to me that was just as much of a retroversion of the theory of what is right in our Government as there could possibly be. Then, after the decision in my case came that of Mrs. Minor, of Missouri. She prosecuted the officers there for denying her the right to vote. She carried her case up to your Supreme Court, and the Supreme Court answered her the same way; that the amendments were made for black men; that their provisions could not protect women; that the Constitution of the United States has no voters of its own.

MRS. SPENCER: And you remember Judge Cartter's decision in my case.

MISS ANTHONY: Mr. Cartter said that women are citizens and may be qualified, &c., but that it requires some sort of legislation to give them the right to vote.

The Congress of the United States notwithstanding, and the Supreme Court of the United States notwithstanding, with all deference and respect, I differ with them all, and know that I am right and that they are wrong. The Constitution of the United States as it is protects me. If I could get a practical application of the Constitution it would protect me and all women in the enjoyment of perfect equality of rights everywhere under the shadow of the American flag.

I do not come to you to petition for special legislation, or for any more amendments to the Constitution, because I think they are unnecessary, but because you say there is not in the Constitution enough to protect me. Therefore I ask that you, true to your own theory and assertion, should go forward to make more constitution.

Let me remind you that in the case of all other classes of citizens under the shadow of our flag you have been true to the theory that taxation and representation are inseparable. Indians not taxed are not counted in the basis of representation, and are not allowed to vote; but the minute that your Indians are counted in the basis of representation and are allowed to vote they are taxed; never before. In my State of New York, and in nearly all the States, the members of the State militia, hundreds and thousands of men, are exempted from taxation on property; in my State to the value of $800, and in most of the States to a value in that neighborhood. While such a member of the militia lives, receives his salary, and is able to earn money, he is exempted; but when he dies the assessor puts his widow's name down upon the assessor's list, and the tax-collector never fails to call upon the widow and make her pay the full tax upon her property. In most of the States clergymen are exempted. In my State of New York they are exempted on property to the value of $1,500. As long as the clergyman lives and receives his fat salary, or his lean one, as the case may be, he is exempted on that amount of property; but when the breath leaves the body of the clergyman, and the widow is left without any income, or without any means of support, the State comes in and taxes the widow.

So it is with regard to all black men. In the State of New York up to the day of the passage of the fifteenth amendment, black men who were willing to remain without reporting themselves worth as much as $250, and thereby to remain without exercising the right to vote, never had their names put on the assessor's list; they were passed by, while, if the poorest colored woman owned 50 feet of real estate, a little cabin anywhere, that colored woman's name was always on the assessor's list, and she was compelled to pay her tax. While Frederick Douglass lived in my State he was never allowed to vote until he could show himself worth the requisite $250; and when he did vote in New York, he voted not because he was a man, not because he was a citizen of the United States, nor yet because he was a citizen of the State, but simply because he was worth the requisite amount of money. In Connecticut both black men and black women were exempted from taxation prior to the adoption of the fifteenth amendment.

The law was amended in 1848, by which black men were thus exempted, and black women followed the same rule in that State. That, I believe, is the only State where black women were exempted from taxation under the law. When the fourteenth and fifteenth amendments were attached to the Constitution they carried to the black man of Connecticut the boon of the ballot as well as the burden of taxation, whereas they carried to the black woman of Connecticut the burden of taxation, but no ballot by which to protect her property. I know a colored woman in New Haven, Conn., worth $50,000, and she never paid a penny of taxation until the ratification of the fifteenth amendment. From that day on she is compelled to pay a heavy tax on that amount of property.

MRS. SPENCER: Is it because she is a citizen? Please explain.

MISS ANTHONY: Because she is black.

MRS. SPENCER: Is it because the fourteenth and fifteenth amendments made women citizens?

MISS ANTHONY: Certainly; because it declared the black people citizens.

Gentlemen, you have before you various propositions of amendment to the Federal Constitution. One is for the election of President by the vote of the people direct. Of course women are not people.

SENATOR EDMUNDS: Angels.

MISS ANTHONY: Yes; angels up in heaven or else devils down there.

SENATOR EDMUNDS: I have never known any of that kind.

MISS ANTHONY: I wish you, gentlemen, would look down there and see the myriads that are there. We want to help them and lift them up. That is exactly the trouble with you, gentlemen; you are forever looking at your own wives, your own mothers, your own sisters, and your own daughters, and they are well cared for and protected; but only look down to the struggling masses of women who have no one to protect them, neither husband, father, brother, son, with no mortal in all the land to protect them. If you would look down there the question would be solved; but the difficulty is that you think only of those who are doing well. We are not speaking for ourselves, but for those who can not speak for themselves. We are speaking for the doomed as much as you, Senator Edmunds, used to speak for the doomed on the plantations in the South.

Amendments have been proposed to put God in the Constitution and to keep God out of the Constitution. All sorts of propositions to amend the Constitution have been made; but I ask that you allow no other amendment to be called the sixteenth but that which shall put into the hands of one-half of the entire people of the nation the right to express their opinions as to how the Constitution shall be amended henceforth. Women have the right to say whether we shall have God in the Constitution as well as men. Women have a right to say whether we shall have a national law or an amendment to the Constitution prohibiting the importation or manufacture of alcoholic liquors. We have a right to have our opinions counted on every possible question concerning the public welfare.

You ask us why we do not get this right to vote first in the school districts, and on school questions, or the questions of liquor license.

It has been shown very clearly why we need something more than that. You have good enough laws to-day in every State in this Union for the suppression of what are termed the social vices; for the suppression of the grog-shops, the gambling houses, the brothels, the obscene shows. There is plenty of legislation in every State in this Union for their suppression if it could be executed. Why is the Government, why are the States and the cities, unable to execute these laws? Simply because there is a large balance of power in every city that does not want those laws executed. Consequently both parties must alike cater to that balance of political power. The party that puts a plank in its platform that the laws against the grog-shops and all the other sinks of iniquity must be executed, is the party that will not get this balance of power to vote for it, and, consequently, the party that can not get into power.

What we ask of you is that you will make of the women of the cities a balance of political power, so that when a mayor, a member of the common council, a supervisor, a justice of the peace, a district attorney, a judge on the bench even, shall go before the people of that city as a candidate for the suffrages of the people he shall not only be compelled to look to the men who frequent the grog-shops, the brothels, and the gambling houses, who will vote for him if he is not in favor of executing the law, but that he shall have to look to the mothers, the sisters, the wives, the daughters of those deluded men to see what they will do if he does not execute the law.

We want to make of ourselves a balance of political power. What we need is the power to execute the laws. We have got laws enough. Let me give you one little fact in regard to my own city of Rochester. You all know how that wonderful whip called the temperance crusade roused the whisky ring. It caused the whisky force to concentrate itself more strongly at the ballot-box than ever before, so that when the report of the elections in the spring of 1874 went over the country the result was that the whisky ring was triumphant, and that the whisky ticket was elected more largely than ever before. Senator Thurman will remember how it was in his own State of Ohio. Everybody knows that if my friends, Mrs. ex-Governor Wallace, Mrs. Allen, and all the women of the great West could have gone to the ballot-box at those municipal elections and voted for candidates, no such result would have occurred; while you refused by the laws of the State to the women the right to have their opinions counted, every rum-seller, every drunkard, every pauper even from the poor-house, and every criminal outside of the State's prison came out on election day to express his opinion and have it counted.

The next result of that political event was that the ring demanded new legislation to protect the whisky traffic everywhere. In my city the women did not crusade the streets, but they said they would help the men to execute the law. They held meetings, sent out committees, and had testimony secured against every man who had violated the law, and when the board of excise held its meeting those women assembled, three or four hundred, in the church one morning, and marched in a solid body to the common council chamber where the board of excise was sitting. As one rum-seller after another brought in his petition for a renewal of license, who had violated the law, those women presented the testimony against him. The law of the State of New York is that no man shall have a renewal who has violated the law. But in not one case did that board refuse to grant a renewal of license because of the testimony which those women presented, and at the close of the sitting it was found that twelve hundred more licenses had been granted than ever before in the history of the State. Then the defeated women said they would have those men punished according to law.

Again they retained an attorney and appointed committees to investigate all over the city. They got the proper officer to prosecute every rum-seller. I was at their meeting. One woman reported that the officer in every city refused to prosecute the liquor dealer who had violated the law. Why? Because if he should do so he would lose the votes of all the employees of certain shops on that street, if another he would lose the votes of the railroad employees, and if another he would lose the German vote, if another the Irish vote, and so on. I said to those women what I say to you, and what I know to be true to-day, that if the women of the city of Rochester had held the power of the ballot in their hands they would have been a great political balance of power.

The last report was from District Attorney Raines. The women complained of a lager-beer-garden keeper. Said the district attorney, "Ladies, you are right, this man is violating the law, everybody knows it, but if I should prosecute him I would lose the entire German vote." Said I, "Ladies, do you not see that if the women of the city of Rochester had the right to vote District Attorney Raines would have been compelled to have stopped and counted, weighed and measured? He would have said, 'If I prosecute that lager-beer German I shall lose the 5,000 German votes in this city, but if I fail to prosecute him and execute the laws I shall lose the votes of 20,000 women.'"

Do you not see, gentlemen, that so long as you put this power of the ballot in the hands of every possible man, rich, poor, drunk, sober, educated, ignorant, outside of the State's prison, to make or unmake, not only every law and lawmaker, but every office-holder who has to do with the executing of the law, and take the power from the hands of the women of the nation, the mothers, you put the long arm of the lever, as we call it in mechanics, in the hands of the whisky power and make it utterly impossible for regulation of sobriety to be maintained in our community? The first step towards social regulation and good society in towns, cities, and villages is the ballot in the hands of the mothers of those places. I appeal to you especially in this matter.

I do not know what you think about the proper sphere of women. It matters little what any of us think about it. We shall each and every individual find our own proper sphere if we are left to act in freedom; but my opinion is that when the whole arena of politics and government is thrown open to women they will endeavor to do very much as they do in their homes; that the men will look after the greenback theory or the hard-money theory, that you will look after free-trade or tariff, and the women will do the home house-keeping of the government, which is to take care of the moral government and the social regulation of our home department.

It seems to me that we have the power of government outside to shape and control circumstances, but that the inside power, the government house-keeping, is powerless, and is compelled to accept whatever conditions or circumstances shall be granted.

Therefore I do not ask for liquor suffrage alone, nor for school suffrage alone, because that would amount to nothing. We must be able to have a voice in the election not only of every law-maker, but of every one who has to do either with the making or the executing of the laws.

Then you ask why we do not get suffrage by the popular-vote method, State by State? I answer, because there is no reason why I, for instance, should desire the women of one State of this nation to vote any more than the women of another State. I have no more interest as regards the women of New York than I have as regards the women of Indiana, Iowa, or any of the States represented by the women who have come up here. The reason why I do not wish to get this right by what you call the popular-vote method, the State vote, is because I believe there is a United States citizenship. I believe that this is a nation, and to be a citizen of this nation should be a guaranty to every citizen of the right to a voice in the Government, and should give to me my right to express my opinion. You deny to me my liberty, my freedom, if you say that I shall have no voice whatever in making, shaping, or controlling the conditions of society in which I live. I differ from Judge Hunt, and I hope I am respectful when I say that I think he made a very funny mistake when he said that fundamental rights belong to the States and only surface rights to the National Government. I hope you will agree with me that the fundamental right of citizenship, the right to voice in the Government, is a national right.

The National Government may concede to the States the right to decide by a majority as to what banks they shall have, what laws they shall enact with regard to insurance, with regard to property, and any other question; but I insist upon it that the National Government should not leave it a question with the States that a majority in any State may disfranchise the minority under any circumstances whatsoever. The franchise to you men is not secure. You hold it to-day, to be sure, by the common consent of white men, but if at any time, on your principle of government, the majority of any of the States should choose to amend the State constitution so as to disfranchise this or that portion of the white men by making this or that condition, by all the decisions of the Supreme Court and by the legislation thus far there is nothing to hinder them.

Therefore the women demand a sixteenth amendment to bring to women the right to vote, or if you please to confer upon women their right to vote, to protect them in it, and to secure men in their right, because you are not secure.

I would let the States act upon almost every other question by majorities, except the power to say whether my opinion shall be counted. I insist upon it that no State shall decide that question.

Then the popular-vote method is an impracticable thing. We tried to get negro suffrage by the popular vote, as you will remember. Senator Thurman will remember that in Ohio the Republicans submitted the question in 1867, and with all the prestige of the national Republican party and of the State party, when every influence that could be brought by the power and the patronage of the party in power was brought to bear, yet negro suffrage ran behind the regular Republican ticket 40,000.

It was tried in Kansas, it was tried in New York, and everywhere that it was submitted the question was voted down overwhelmingly. Just so we tried to get women suffrage by the popular-vote method in Kansas in 1867, in Michigan in 1874, in Colorado in 1877, and in each case the result was precisely the same, the ratio of the vote standing one-third for women suffrage and two-thirds against women suffrage. If we were to canvass State after State we should get no better vote than that. Why? Because the question of the enfranchisement of women is a question of government, a question of philosophy, of understanding, of great fundamental principle, and the masses of the hard-working people of this nation, men and women, do not think upon principles. They can only think on the one eternal struggle wherewithal to be fed, to be clothed, and to be sheltered. Therefore I ask you not to compel us to have this question settled by what you term the popular-vote method.

Let me illustrate by Colorado, the most recent State, in the election of 1877. I am happy to say to you that I have canvassed three States for this question. If Senator Chandler were alive, or if Senator Ferry were in this room, they would remember that I followed in their train in Michigan, with larger audiences than either of those Senators throughout the whole canvass. I want to say, too, that although those Senators may have believed in woman suffrage, they did not say much about it. They did not help us much. The Greenback movement was quite popular in Michigan at that time. The Republicans and Greenbackers made a most humble bow to the grangers, but women suffrage did not get much help. In Colorado, at the close of the canvass, 6,666 men voted "Yes." Now I am going to describe the men who voted "Yes." They were native-born white men, temperance men, cultivated, broad, generous, just men, men who think. On the other hand, 16,007 voted "No."

Now I am going to describe that class of voters. In the southern part of that State there are Mexicans, who speak the Spanish language. They put their wheat in circles on the ground with the heads out, and drive a mule around to thrash it. The vast population of Colorado is made up of that class of people. I was sent out to speak in a voting precinct having 200 voters; 150 of those voters were Mexican greasers, 40 of them foreign-born citizens, and just 10 of them were born in this country; and I was supposed to be competent to convert those men to let me have as much right in this Government as they had, when, unfortunately, the great majority of them could not understand a word that I said. Fifty or sixty Mexican greasers stood against the wall with their hats down over their faces. The Germans put seats in a lager-beer saloon, and would not attend unless I made a speech there; so I had a small audience.

MRS. ARCHIBALD: There is one circumstance that I should like to relate. In the county of Las Animas, a county where there is a large population of Mexicans, and where they always have a large majority over the native population, they do not know our language at all. Consequently a number of tickets must be printed for those people in Spanish. The gentleman in our little town of Trinidad who had the charge of the printing of those tickets, being adverse to us, had every ticket printed against woman suffrage. The samples that were sent to us from Denver were "for" or "against," but the tickets that were printed only had the word "against" on them, so that our friends had to scratch their tickets, and all those Mexican people who could not understand this trick and did not know the facts of the case, voted against woman suffrage; so that we lost a great many votes. This was man's generosity.

MISS ANTHONY: Special legislation for the benefit of woman! I will admit you that on the floor of the constitutional convention was a representative Mexican, intelligent, cultivated, chairman of the committee on suffrage, who signed the petition, and was the first to speak in favor of woman suffrage. Then they have in Denver about four hundred negroes. Governor Routt said to me, "The four hundred Denver negroes are going to vote solid for woman suffrage." I said, "I do not know much about the Denver negroes, but I know certainly what all negroes were educated in, and slavery never educated master or negro into a comprehension of the great principles of human freedom of our nation; it is not possible, and I do not believe they are going to vote for us." Just ten of those Denver negroes voted for woman suffrage. Then, in all the mines of Colorado the vast majority of wage laborers, as you know, are foreigners.

There may be intelligent foreigners in this country, and I know there are, who are in favor of the enfranchisement of woman, but that one does not happen to be Carl Schurz, I am ashamed to say. And I want to say to you of Carl Schurz, that side by side with that man on the battlefield of Germany was Madame Anneke, as noble a woman as ever trod the American soil. She rode by the side of her husband, who was an officer, on the battlefield; she slept in battlefield tents, and she fled from Germany to this country, for her life and property, side by side with Carl Schurz. Now, what is it for Carl Schurz, stepping up to the very door of the Presidency and looking back to Madame Anneke, who fought for liberty as well as he, to say, "You be subject in this Republic; I will be sovereign." If it is an insult for Carl Schurz to say that to a foreign-born woman, what is it for him to say it to Mrs. ex-Governor Wallace, Elizabeth Cady Stanton, Lucretia Mott—to the native-born, educated, tax-paying women in this Republic? I can forgive an ignorant foreigner; I can forgive an ignorant negro; but I can not forgive Carl Schurz.

Right in the file of the foreigners opposed to woman suffrage, educated under monarchical governments that do not comprehend our principles, whom I have seen traveling through the prairies of Iowa or the prairies of Minnesota, are the Bohemians, Swedes, Norwegians, Germans, Irishmen, Mennonites; I have seen them riding on those magnificent loads of wheat with those magnificent Saxon horses, shining like glass on a sunny morning, every one of them going to vote "no" against woman suffrage. You can not convert them; it is impossible. Now and then there is a whisky manufacturer, drunkard, inebriate, libertine, and what we call a fast man, and a colored man, broad and generous enough to be willing to let women vote, to let his mother have her opinion counted as to whether there shall be license or no license, but the rank and file of all classes who wish to enjoy full license in what are termed the petty vices of men are pitted solid against the enfranchisement of women.

Then, in addition to all these, there are, as you know, a few religious bigots left in the world who really believe that somehow or other if women are allowed to vote St. Paul would feel badly about it. I do not know but that some of the gentlemen present belong to that class. So, when you put those best men of the nation, having religion about everything except on this one question, whose prejudices control them, with all this vast mass of ignorant, uneducated, degraded population in this country, you make an overwhelming and insurmountable majority against the enfranchisement of women.

It is because of this fact that I ask you not to remand us back to the States, but submit to the States the proposition of a sixteenth amendment. The popular-vote method is not only of itself an impossibility, but it is too humiliating a process to compel the women of this nation to submit to any longer.

I am going to give you an illustration, not because I have any disrespect for the person, because on many other questions he was really a good deal better than a good many other men who had not so bad a name in this nation. When, under the old *régime*, John Morrissey, of my State, the king of gamblers, was a Representative on the floor of Congress, it was humiliating enough for Lucretia Mott, for Elizabeth Cady Stanton, for all of us to come down here to Washington and beg at the feet of John Morrissey that he would let intelligent, native-born women vote, and let us have as much right in this Government and in the government of the city of New York as he had. When John Morrissey was a member of the New York State Legislature it would have been humiliating enough for us to go to the New York State Legislature and pray of John Morrissey to vote to ratify the sixteenth amendment, giving us the right to vote; but if instead of a sixteenth amendment you tell us to go back to the popular-vote method, the old-time method, and go down into John Morrissey's seventh Congressional district in the city of New York, and there, in the sloughs and slums of that great Sodom, in the grog-shops, the gambling-houses, and the brothels, beg at the feet of each individual fisticuff of his constituency to give the noble, educated, native-born, tax-paying women of the State of New York as much right as he has, that would be too bitter a pill for a native-born woman to swallow any longer.

I beg you, gentlemen, to save us from the mortification and the humiliation of appealing to the rabble. We already have on our side the vast majority of the better educated—the best classes of men. You will remember that Senator Christiancy, of Michigan, two years ago, said on the floor of the Senate that of the 40,000 men who voted for woman suffrage in Michigan it was said that there was not a drunkard, not a libertine, not a gambler, not a depraved, low man among them. Is not that something that tells for us, and for our right? It is the fact, in every State of the Union, that we have the intelligent lawyers and the most liberal ministers of all the sects, not excepting the Roman Catholics. A Roman Catholic priest preached a sermon the other day, in which he said, "God grant that there were a thousand Susan B. Anthonys in this city to vote and work for temperance." When a Catholic priest says that there is a great moral necessity pressing down upon this nation demanding the enfranchisement of women, I ask you that you shall not drive us back to beg our rights at the feet of the most ignorant and depraved men of the nation, but that you, the representative men of the nation, will hold the question in the hollow of your hands. We ask you to lift this question out of the hands of the rabble.

You who are here upon the floor of Congress in both Houses are the picked men of the nation. You may say what you please about John Morrissey, the gambler, &c.: he was head and shoulders above the rank and file of his constituency. The world may gabble ever so much about members of Congress being corrupt and being bought and sold; they are as a rule head and shoulders among the great majority who compose their State governments. There is no doubt about it. Therefore I ask of you, as representative men, as men who think, as men who study, as men who philosophize, as men who know, that you will not drive us back to the States any more, but that you will carry out this method of procedure which has been practiced from the beginning of the Government; that is, that you will put a prohibitory amendment in the Constitution and submit the proposition to the several State legislatures. The amendment which has been presented before you reads:

ARTICLE XVI

SECTION 1. The right of suffrage in the United States shall be based on citizenship, and the right of citizens of the United States to vote shall not be denied or abridged by the United States, or by any State, on account of sex, or for any reason not equally applicable to all citizens of the United States.

SECTION 2. Congress shall have power to enforce this article by appropriate legislation.

In this way we would get the right of suffrage just as much by what you call the consent of the States, or the States' rights method, as by any other method. The only point is that it is a decision by the representative men of the States instead of by the rank and file of the ignorant men of the States. If you would submit this proposition for a sixteenth amendment, by a two-thirds vote of the two Houses to the several legislatures, and the several legislatures ratify it, that would be just as much by the consent of the States as if Tom, Dick, and Harry voted "yes" or "no." Is it not, Senator? I want to talk to Democrats as well as Republicans, to show that it is a States' rights method.

SENATOR EDMUNDS: Does anybody propose any other, in case it is done at all by the nation?

MISS ANTHONY: Not by the nation, but they are continually driving us back to get it from the States, State by State. That is the point I want to make. We do not want you to drive us back to the States. We want you men to take the question out of the hands of the rabble of the State.

THE CHAIRMAN: May I interrupt you?

MISS ANTHONY: Yes, sir, I wish you would.

THE CHAIRMAN: You have reflected on this subject a great deal. You think there is a majority, as I understand, even in the State of New York, against women suffrage?

MISS ANTHONY: Yes, sir; overwhelmingly.

THE CHAIRMAN: How, then, would you get Legislatures elected to ratify such a constitutional amendment?

MISS ANTHONY: That brings me exactly to the point.

THE CHAIRMAN: That is the point I wish to hear you upon.

MISS ANTHONY: Because the members of the State Legislatures are intelligent men and can vote and enact laws embodying great principles of the government without in anywise endangering their positions with their constituencies. A constituency composed of ignorant men would vote solid against us because they have never thought on the question. Every man or woman who believes in the enfranchisement of women is educated out of every idea that he or she was born into. We were all born into the idea that the proper sphere of women is subjection, and it takes education and thought and culture to lift us out of it. Therefore when men go to the ballot-box they all vote "no," unless they have actual argument on it. I will illustrate. We have six Legislatures in the nation, for instance, that have extended the right to vote on school questions to the women, and not a single member of the State Legislature has ever lost his office or forfeited the respect or confidence of his constituents as a representative because he voted to give women the right to vote on school questions. It is a question that the unthinking masses never have thought upon. They do not care about it one way or the other, only they have an instinctive feeling that because women never did vote therefore it is wrong that they ever should vote.

MRS. SPENCER: Do make the point that the Congress of the United States leads the Legislatures of the States and educates them.

MISS ANTHONY: When you, representative men, carry this matter to Legislatures, State by State, they will ratify it. My point is that you can safely do this. Senator Thurman, of Ohio, would not lose a single vote in Ohio in voting in favor of the enfranchisement of women. Senator Edmunds would not lose a single Republican vote in the State of Vermont if he puts himself on our side, which, I think, he will do. It is not a political question. We are no political power that can make or break either party to-day. Consequently each man is left independent to express his own moral and intellectual convictions on the matter without endangering himself politically.

SENATOR EDMUNDS: I think, Miss Anthony, you ought to put it on rather higher, I will not say stronger, ground. If you can convince us that it is right we would not stop to see how it affected us politically.

MISS ANTHONY: I was coming to that, I was going to say to all of you men in office here to-day that if you can not go forward and carry out either your Democratic or your Republican or your Greenback theories, for instance, on the finance, there is no great political power that is going to take you away from these halls and prevent you from doing all those other things which you want to do, and you can act out your own moral and intellectual convictions on this without let or hindrance.

SENATOR EDMUNDS: Without any danger to the public interests, you mean.

MISS ANTHONY: Without any danger to the public interests. I did not mean to make a bad insinuation, Senator.

I want to give you another reason why we appeal to you. In these three States where the question has been submitted and voted down we can not get another Legislature to resubmit it, because they say the people have expressed their opinion and decided no, and therefore nobody with any political sense would resubmit the question. It is therefore impossible in any one of those States. We have tried hard in Kansas for ten years to get the question resubmitted; the vote of that State seems to be taken as a finality. We ask you to lift the sixteenth Amendment out of the arena of the public mass into the arena of thinking legislative brains, the brains of the nation, under the law and the Constitution. Not only do we ask it for that purpose, but when you will have by a two-thirds vote submitted the proposition to the several Legislatures, you have put the pin down and it never can go back. No subsequent Congress can revoke that submission of the proposition; there will be so much gained; it can not slide back. Then we will go to New York or to Pennsylvania, and urge upon the Legislatures the ratification of that amendment. They may refuse; they may vote it down the first time. Then we will go to the next Legislature, and the next Legislature, and plead and plead, from year to year, if it takes ten years. It is an open question to every Legislature until we can get one that will ratify it, and when that Legislature has once voted and ratified it no subsequent legislation can revoke their ratification.

Thus, you perceive, Senators, that every step we would gain by this sixteenth amendment process is fast and not to be done over again. That is why I appeal to you especially. As I have shown you in the respective States, if we fail to educate the people of a whole State— and in Michigan it was only six months, and in Colorado less than six months—the State Legislatures say that is the end of it. I appeal to you, therefore, to adopt the course that we suggest.

Gentlemen of the committee, if there is a question that you want to ask me before I make my final appeal, I should like to have you put it now; any question as to constitutional law or your right to go forward. Of course you do not deny to us that this amendment will be right in the line of all the amendments heretofore. The eleventh, twelfth, thirteenth, fourteenth, fifteenth amendments are all in line prohibiting the States from doing something which they heretofore thought they had a right to do. Now we ask you to prohibit the States from denying to women their rights.

I want to show you in closing that of the great acts of justice done during the war and since the war the first one was a great military necessity. We never got one inch of headway in putting down the rebellion until the purpose of this great nation was declared that slavery should be abolished. Then, as if by magic, we went forward and put down the rebellion. At the close of the rebellion the nation stood again at a perfect deadlock. The Republican party was trembling in the balance, because it feared that it could not hold its position, until it should have secured by legislation to the Government what it had gained at the point of the sword, and when the nation declared its purpose to enfranchise the negro it was a political necessity. I do not want to take too much vainglory out of the heads of Republicans, but nevertheless it is a great national fact that neither of those great acts of beneficence to the negro race was done because of any high, over-shadowing moral conviction on the part of any considerable minority even of the people of this nation, but simply because of a military necessity slavery was abolished, and simply because of a political necessity black men were enfranchised.

The blackest Republican State you had voted down negro suffrage, and that was Kansas in 1867; Michigan voted it down in 1867; Ohio voted it down in 1867. Iowa was the only State that ever voted negro suffrage by a majority of the citizens to which the question was submitted, and they had not more than seventy-five negroes in the whole State; so it was not a very practical question. Therefore, it may be fairly said, I think, that it was a military necessity that compelled one of those acts of justice, and a political necessity that compelled the other.

It seems to me that from the first word uttered by our dear friend, Mrs. ex-Governor Wallace, of Indiana, all the way down, we have been presenting to you the fact that there is a great moral necessity pressing upon this nation to-day, that you shall go forward and attach a sixteenth amendment to the Federal Constitution which shall put in the hands of the women of this nation the power to help make, shape, and control the social conditions of society everywhere. I appeal to you from that standpoint that you shall submit this proposition.

There is one other point to which I want to call your attention. The Senate Judiciary Committee, Senator Edmunds chairman, reported that the United States could do nothing to protect women in the right to vote under the amendments. Now I want to give you a few points where the United States interferes to take away the right to vote from women where the State has given it to them. In Wyoming, for instance, by a Democratic legislature, the women were enfranchised. They were not only allowed to vote but to sit upon juries, the same as men. Those of you who read the reports giving the results of that action have not forgotten that the first result of women sitting upon juries was that wherever there was a violation of the whisky law they brought in verdicts accordingly for the execution of the law; and you will remember, too, that the first man who ever had a verdict of guilty for murder in the first degree in that Territory was tried by a jury made up largely of women. Always up to that day every jury had brought in a verdict of shot in self-defense, although the person shot down may have been entirely unarmed. Then, in cities like Cheyenne and Laramie, persons entered complaints against keepers of houses of ill-fame.

Women were on the jury, and the result was in every case that before the juries could bring in a bill of indictment the women had taken the train and left the town. Why do you hear no more of women sitting on juries in that Territory? Simply because the United States marshal, who is appointed by the President to go to Wyoming, refuses to put the names of women into the box from which the jury is drawn. There the United States Government interferes to take the right away.

A DELEGATE: I should like to state that Governor Hoyt, of Wyoming, who was the governor who signed the act giving to women this right, informed me that the right had been restored, and that his sister, who resides there, recently served on a jury.

MISS ANTHONY: I am glad to hear it. It is two years since I was there, but I was told that that was the case. In Utah the women were given the right to vote, but a year and a half ago their Legislative Assembly found that although they had the right to vote the Territorial law provided that only male voters should hold office. The Legislative Assembly of Utah passed a bill providing that women should be eligible to all the offices of the Territory. The school offices, superintendents of schools, were the offices in particular to which the women wanted to be elected. Governor Emory, appointed by the President of the United States, vetoed that bill. Thus the full operations of enfranchisement conferred by two of the Territories has been stopped by Federal interference.

You ask why I come here instead of going to the State Legislatures. You say that whenever the Legislatures extend the right of suffrage to us by the constitutions of their States we can get it. Massachusetts, New Hampshire, Minnesota, Colorado, Kansas, Oregon, all these States, have had the school suffrage extended by legislative enactment. If the question had been submitted to the rank and file of the people of Boston, with 66,000 men paying nothing but the poll-tax, they would have undoubtedly voted against letting women have the right to vote for members of the school board; but their intelligent representatives on the floor of the Legislature voted in favor of the extension of the school suffrage to the women. The first result in Boston has been the election of quite a number of women to the school board. In Minnesota, in the little town of Rochester, the school board declared its purpose to cut the women teachers' wages down. It did not propose to touch the principal, who was a man, but they proposed to cut all the women down from $50 to $35. One woman put her bonnet on and went over the entire town and said, "We have got a right to vote for this school board, and let us do so." They all turned out and voted, and not a single $35 man was re-elected, but all those who were in favor of paying $50.

It seems to be a sort of charity to let a woman teach school. You say here that if a woman has a father, mother, or brother, or anybody to support her, she can not have a place in the Departments. In the city of Rochester they cannot let a married woman teach school because she has got a husband, and it is supposed he ought to support her. The women are working in the Departments, as everywhere else, for half price, and the only pretext, you tell us, for keeping women there is because the Government can economize by employing women for less money. The other day when I saw a newspaper item stating that the Government proposed to compensate Miss Josephine Meeker for all her bravery, heroism, and terrible sufferings by giving her a place in the Interior Department, it made my blood boil to the ends of my fingers and toes. To give that girl a chance to work in the Department; to do just as much work as a man, and pay her half as much, was a charity. That was a beneficence on the part of this grand Government to her. We want the ballot for bread. When we do equal work we want equal wages.

MRS. SAXON: California, in her recent convention, prohibits the Legislature hereafter from enacting any law for woman's suffrage, does it not?

MISS ANTHONY: I do not know. I have not seen the new constitution.

MRS. SAXON: It does. The convention inserted a provision in the constitution that the Legislature could not act upon the subject at all.

MISS ANTHONY: Everywhere that we have gone, Senators, to ask our right at the hands of any legislative or political body, we have been the subjects of ridicule. For instance, I went before the great national Democratic convention in New York, in 1868, as a delegate from the New York Woman Suffrage Association, to ask that great party, now that it wanted to come to the front again, to put a genuine Jeffersonian plank in its platform, pledging the ballot to all citizens, women as well as men, should it come into power. You may remember how Mr. Seymour ordered my petition to be read, after looking at it in the most scrutinizing manner, when it was referred to the committee on resolutions, where it has slept the sleep of death from that day to this. But before the close of the convention a body of ignorant workingmen sent in a petition clamoring for greenbacks, and you remember that the Democratic party bought those men by putting a solid greenback plank in the platform.

Everybody supposed they would nominate Pendleton, or some other man of pronounced views, but instead of doing that they nominated Horatio Seymour, who stood on the fence, politically speaking. My friends, Mrs. Stanton, Lucretia Mott, and women who have brains and education, women who are tax-payers, went there and petitioned for the practical application of the fundamental principles of our Government to one-half of the people. Those most ignorant workingmen, the vast mass of them foreigners, went there, and petitioned that that great political party should favor greenbacks.

Why did they treat those workingmen with respect, and put a green-back plank in their platform, and only table us, and ignore us? Simply because the workingmen represented the power of the ballot. They could make or unmake the great Democratic party at that election. The women were powerless. We could be ridiculed and ignored with impunity, and so we were laughed at, and put on the table.

Then the Republicans went to Chicago, and they did just the same thing. They said the Government bonds must be paid in precisely the currency specified by the Congressional enactment, and Talleyrand himself could not have devised how not to say anything better than the Republicans did at Chicago on that question. Then they nominated a man who had not any financial opinions whatever, and who was not known, except for his military record, and they went into the campaign. Both those parties had this petition from us.

I met a woman in Grand Rapids, Mich., a short time ago. She came to me one morning and told me about the obscene shows licensed in that city, and said that she thought of memorializing the Legislature. I said, "Do; you can not do anything else; you are helpless, but you can petition. Of course they will laugh at you." Notwithstanding, I drew up a petition and she circulated it. Twelve hundred of the best citizens signed that petition, and the lady carried it to the Legislature, just as Mrs. Wallace took her petition in the Indiana Legislature. They read it, laughed at it, and laid it on the table; and at the close of the session, by a unanimous vote, they retired in a solid body to witness the obscene show themselves. After witnessing it, they not only allowed the license to continue for that year, but they have licensed it every year from that day to this, against all the protests of the petitioners.

SENATOR EDMUNDS: Do not think we are wanting in respect to you and the ladies here because you say something that makes us laugh.

MISS ANTHONY: You are not laughing at me; you are treating me respectfully, because you are hearing my argument; you are not asleep, not one of you, and I am delighted.

Now, I am going to tell you one other fact. Seven thousand of the best citizens of Illinois petitioned the Legislature of 1877 to give them the poor privilege of voting on the license question. A gentleman presented their petition; the ladies were in the lobbies around the room. A gentleman made a motion that the president of the State association of the Christian Temperance Union be allowed to address the Legislature regarding the petition of the memorialists, when a gentleman sprang to his feet, and said it was well enough for the honorable gentleman to present the petition, and have it received and laid on the table, but "for a gentleman to rise in his seat and propose that the valuable time of the honorable gentlemen of the Illinois Legislature should be consumed in discussing the nonsense of those women is going a little too far. I move that the sergeant-at-arms be ordered to clear the hall of the house of representatives of the mob;" referring to those Christian women. Now, they had had the lobbyists of the whisky ring in that Legislature for years and years, not only around it at respectful distances, but inside the bar, and nobody ever made a motion to clear the halls of the whisky mob there. It only takes Christian women to make a mob.

MRS. SAXON: We were treated extremely respectfully in Louisiana. It showed plainly the temper of the convention when the present governor admitted that woman suffrage was a fact bound to come. They gave us the privilege of having women on the school boards, but then the officers are appointed by men who are politicians.

MISS ANTHONY: I want to read a few words that come from good authority, for black men at least. I find here a little extract that I copied years ago from the Anti-Slavery Standard of 1870. As you know, Wendell Phillips was the editor of that paper at that time:

"A man with the ballot in his hand is the master of the situation. He defines all his other rights; what is not already given him he takes."

That is exactly what we want, Senators. The rights you have not already given us; we want to get in such a position that we can take them.

"The ballot makes every class sovereign over its own fate. Corruption may steal from a man his independence; capital may starve, and intrigue fetter him, at times; but against all these, his vote, intelligently and honestly cast, is, in the long run, his full protection. If, in the struggle, his fort surrenders, it is only because it is betrayed from within. No power ever permanently wronged a voting class without its own consent."

Senators, I want to ask of you that you will, by the law and parliamentary rules of your committee, allow us to agitate this question by publishing this report and the report which you shall make upon our petitions, as I hope you will make a report. If your committee is so pressed with business that it can not possibly consider and report upon this question, I wish some of you would make a motion on the floor of the Senate that a special committee be appointed to take the whole question of the enfranchisement of women into consideration, and that that committee shall have nothing else to do. This off-year of politics, when there is nothing to do but to try how not to do it (politically, I mean, I am not speaking personally), is the best time you can have to consider the question of woman suffrage, and I ask you to use your influence with the Senate to have it specially attended to this year. Do not make us come here thirty years longer. It is twelve years since the first time I came before a Senate committee. I said then to Charles Sumner, if I could make the honorable Senator from Massachusetts believe that I feel the degradation and the humiliation of disfranchisement precisely as he would if his fellows had adjudged him incompetent from any cause whatever from having his opinion counted at the ballot-box we should have our right to vote in the twinkling of an eye.

Elizabeth Cady Stanton

(1815–1902)

THE SOLITUDE OF SELF
January 18, 1892

Elizabeth Cady Stanton was one of the leading figures of the American women's rights movement of the nineteenth century. Along with Lucretia Mott, Stanton was the driving force behind the 1848 Seneca Falls Women's Rights Convention, where she presented her "Declaration of Sentiments," a document modeled after the Declaration of Independence, which asserted women's civil, social, religious, and political rights. The following speech, delivered on January 18, 1892, to the Committee of the Judiciary of the United States Congress, marked the end of Stanton's long career, appealing one last time for the rights that she had spent her life working to achieve.

MR. CHAIRMAN and gentlemen of the Committee: We have been speaking before Committees of the Judiciary for the last twenty years, and we have gone over all the arguments in favor of the sixteenth amendment which are familiar to all you gentlemen; therefore, it will not be necessary that I should repeat them again.

The point I wish plainly to bring before you on this occasion is the individuality of each human soul; our Protestant idea, the right of individual conscience and judgment—our republican idea, individual citizenship. In discussing the rights of woman, we are to consider, first, what belongs to her as an individual, in a world of her own, the arbiter of her own destiny, an imaginary Robinson Crusoe with her woman Friday on a solitary island. Her rights under such circumstances are to use all her faculties for her own safety and happiness.

Secondly, if we consider her as a citizen, as a member of a great nation, she must have the same rights as all other members, according to the fundamental principles of our government.

Thirdly, viewed as a woman, an equal factor in civilization, her rights and duties are still the same—individual happiness and development.

Fourthly, it is only the incidental relations of life, such as mother, wife, sister, daughter, that may involve some special duties and training. In the usual discussion in regard to woman's sphere, such men as Herbert Spencer, Frederic Harrison, and Grant Allen uniformly subordinate her rights and duties as an individual, as a citizen, as a woman, to the necessities of these incidental relations, some of which a large class of women may never assume. In discussing the sphere of man we do not decide his rights as an individual, as a citizen, as a man by his duties as a father, a husband, a brother, or a son, relations some of which he may never fill. Moreover he would be better fitted for these very relations and whatever special work he might choose to do to earn his bread by the complete development of all his faculties as an individual.

Just so with woman. The education that will fit her to discharge the duties in the largest sphere of human usefulness will best fit her for whatever special work she may be compelled to do.

The insolation of every human soul and the necessity of self-dependence must give each individual the right, to choose his own surroundings.

The strongest reason for giving woman all the opportunities for higher education, for the full development of her faculties, forces of mind and body for giving her the most enlarged freedom of thought and action; a complete emancipation from all forms of bondage, of custom, dependence, superstition; from all the crippling influences of fear, is the solitude and personal responsibility of her own individual life. The strongest reason why we ask for woman a voice in the government under which she lives; in the religion she is asked to believe; equality in social life, where she is the chief factor; a place in the trades and professions, where she may earn her bread, is because of her birthright to self-sovereignty; because, as an individual, she must rely on herself. No matter how much women prefer to lean, to be protected and supported, nor how much men desire to have them do so, they must make the voyage of life alone, and for safety in an emergency they must know something of the laws of navigation. To guide our own craft, we must be captain, pilot, engineer; with chart and compass to stand at the wheel; to watch the wind and waves and know when to take in the sail, and to read the signs in the firmament over all. It matters not whether the solitary voyager is man or woman.

Nature having endowed them equally, leaves them to their own skill and judgment in the hour of danger, and, if not equal to the occasion, alike they perish.

To appreciate the importance of fitting every human soul for independent action, think for a moment of the immeasurable solitude of self. We come into the world alone, unlike all who have gone before us; we leave it alone under circumstances peculiar to ourselves. No mortal ever has been, no mortal ever will be like the soul just launched on the sea of life. There can never again be just such environments as make up the infancy, youth and manhood of this one. Nature never repeats herself, and the possibilities of one human soul will never be found in another. No one has ever found two blades of ribbon grass alike, and no one will ever find two human beings alike. Seeing, then, what must be the infinite diversity in human character, we can in a measure appreciate the loss to a nation when any large class of the people is uneducated and unrepresented in the government. We ask for the complete development of every individual, first, for his own benefit and happiness. In fitting out an army we give each soldier his own knapsack, arms, powder, his blanket, cup, knife, fork and spoon. We provide alike for all their individual necessities, then each man bears his own burden.

Again we ask complete individual development for the general good; for the consensus of the competent on the whole round of human interest; on all questions of national life, and here each man must bear his share of the general burden. It is sad to see how soon friendless children are left to bear their own burdens before they can analyze their feelings; before they can even tell their joys and sorrows, they are thrown on their own resources. The great lesson that nature seems to teach us at all ages is self-dependence, self-protection, self-support. What a touching instance of a child's solitude; of that hunger of heart for love and recognition, in the case of a little girl who helped to dress a christmas tree for the children of the family in which she served. On finding there was no present for herself she slipped away in the darkness and spent the night in an open field sitting on a stone, and when found in the morning was weeping as if her heart would break. No mortal will ever know the thoughts that passed through the mind of the friendless child in the long hours of that cold night, with only the silent stars to keep her company. The mention of her case in the daily papers moved many generous hearts to send her presents, but in the hours of her keenest sufferings she was thrown wholly on herself for consolation.

In youth our most bitter disappointments, our brightest hopes and ambitions are known only to ourselves; even our friendship and love we never fully share with another; there is something of every passion in every situation we conceal. Even so in our triumphs and our defeats.

The successful candidate for Presidency and his opponent each have a solitude peculiarly his own, and good form forbids either to speak of his pleasure or regret. The solitude of the king on his throne and the prisoner in his cell differs in characters and degree, but it is solitude nevertheless.

We ask no sympathy from others in the anxiety and agony of a broken friendship or shattered love. When death sunders our nearest ties, alone we sit in the shadows of our affliction. Alike mid the greatest triumphs and darkest tragedies of life we walk alone. On the divine heights of human attainments, eulogized and worshipped as a hero or saint, we stand alone. In ignorance, poverty, and vice, as a pauper or criminal, alone we starve or steal; alone we suffer the sneers and rebuffs of our fellows; alone we are hunted and hounded through dark courts and alleys, in by-ways and highways; alone we stand in the judgment seat; alone in the prison cell we lament our crimes and misfortunes; alone we expiate them on the gallows. In hours like these we realize the awful solitude of individual life, its pains, its penalties, its responsibilities; hours in which the youngest and most helpless are thrown on their own resources for guidance and consolation. Seeing then that life must ever be a march and a battle, that each soldier must be equipped for his own protection, it is the height of cruelty to rob the individual of a single natural right.

To throw obstacles in the way of a complete education is like putting out the eyes; to deny the rights of property, like cutting off the hands. To deny political equality is to rob the ostracised of all self-respect; of credit in the market place; of recompense in the world of work; of a voice in those who make and administer the law; a choice in the jury before whom they are tried, and in the judge who decides their punishment. Shakespeare's play Titus and Andronicus contains a terrible satire on woman's position in the nineteenth century—"Rude men" (the play tells us) "seized the king's daughter, cut out her tongue, cut off her hands, and then bade her go call for water and wash her hands." What a picture of woman's position. Robbed of her natural rights, handicapped by law and custom at every turn, yet compelled to fight her own battles, and in the emergencies of life to fall back on herself for protection.

The girl of sixteen, thrown on the world to support herself, to make her own place in society, to resist the temptations that surround her and maintain a spotless integrity, must do all this by native force or superior education. She does not acquire this power by being trained to trust others and distrust herself. If she wearies of the struggle, finding it hard work to swim upstream, and allows herself to drift with the current, she will find plenty of company, but not one to share her misery in the hour of her deepest humiliation. If she tries to retrieve her position, to conceal the past, her life is hedged about with fears lest willing hands should tear the veil from what she fain would hide. Young and friendless, she knows the bitter solitude of self.

How the little courtesies of life on the surface of society, deemed so important from man towards woman, fade into utter insignificance in view of the deeper tragedies in which she must play her part alone, where no human aid is possible.

The young wife and mother, at the head of some establishment with a kind husband to shield her from the adverse winds of life, with wealth, fortune, and position, has a certain harbor of safety, secure against the ordinary ills of life. But to manage a household, have a desirable influence in society, keep her friends and the affections of her husband, train her children and servants well, she must have rare common sense, wisdom, diplomacy, and a knowledge of human nature. To do all this she needs the cardinal virtues and the strong points of character that the most successful stateman possesses.

An uneducated woman, trained to dependence, with no resources in herself must make a failure of any position in life. But society says women do not need a knowledge of the world; the liberal training that experience in public life must give, all the advantages of collegiate education; but when for the lack of all this, the woman's happiness is wrecked, alone she bears her humiliation; and the solitude of the weak and the ignorant is indeed pitiful. In the wild chase for the prizes of life they are ground to powder.

In age, when the pleasures of youth are passed, children grown up, married and gone, the hurry and bustle of life in a measure over, when the hands are weary of active service, when the old armchair and the fireside are the chosen resorts, then men and women alike must fall back on their own resources. If they cannot find companionship in books, if they have no interest in the vital questions of the hour, no interest in watching the consummation of reforms, with which they might have been identified, they soon pass into their dotage. The more fully the faculties of the mind are developed and kept in use, the longer the period of vigor and active interest in all around us continues. If from a lifelong participation in public affairs a woman feels responsible for the laws regulating our system of education, the discipline of our jails and prisons, the sanitary conditions of our private homes, public buildings, and thoroughfares, an interest in commerce, finance, our foreign relations, in any or all these questions, her solitude will at least be respectable, and she will not be driven to gossip or scandal for entertainment.

The chief reason for opening to every soul the doors to the whole round of human duties and pleasures is the individual development thus attained, the resources thus provided under all circumstances to mitigate the solitude that at times must come to everyone. I once asked Prince Krapotkin, the Russian nihilist, how he endured his long years in prison, deprived of books, pen, ink, and paper. "Ah," he said, "I thought out many questions on which I had a deep interest. In the pursuit of an idea I took no note of time. When tired of solving knotty problems I recited all the beautiful passages in prose or verse I had ever learned. I became acquainted with myself and my own resources. I had a world of my own, a vast empire, that no Russian jailor or Czar could invade." Such is the value of liberal thought and broad culture when shut from all human companionship, bringing comfort and sunshine within even the four walls of a prison cell.

As women ofttimes share a similar fate, should they not have all the consolation that the most liberal education can give? Their suffering in the prisons of St. Petersburg; in the long, weary marches to Siberia, and in the mines, working side by side with men, surely call for all the self-support that the most exalted sentiments of heroism can give. When suddenly roused at midnight, with the startling cry of "fire! fire!" to find the house over their heads in flames, do women wait for men to point the way to safety? And are the men, equally bewildered and half suffocated with smoke, in a position to more than save themselves?

At such times the most timid women have shown a courage and heroism in saving their husbands and children that has surprised everybody. Inasmuch, then, as woman shares equally the joys and sorrows of time and eternity, is it not the height of presumption in man to propose to represent her at the ballot box and the throne of grace, do her voting in the state, her praying in the church, and to assume the position of high priest at the family altar.

Nothing strengthens the judgment and quickens the conscience like individual responsibility. Nothing adds such dignity to character as the recognition of one's self-sovereignty; the right to an equal place, every where conceded; a place earned by personal merit, not an artificial attainment, by inheritance, wealth, family, and position. Seeing, then that the responsibilities of life rests equally on man and woman, that their destiny is the same, they need the same preparation for time and eternity. The talk of sheltering woman from the fierce storms of life is the sheerest mockery, for they beat on her from every point of the compass, just as they do on man, and with more fatal results, for he has been trained to protect himself, to resist, to conquer. Such are the facts in human experience, the responsibilities of individual sovereignty. Rich and poor, intelligent and ignorant, wise and foolish, virtuous and vicious, man and woman, it is ever the same, each soul must depend wholly on itself.

Whatever the theories may be of woman's dependence on man, in the supreme moments of her life he can not bear her burdens. Alone she goes to the gates of death to give life to every man that is born into the world. No one can share her fears, no one can mitigate her pangs; and if her sorrow is greater than she can bear, alone she passes beyond the gates into the vast unknown.

From the mountain tops of Judea, long ago, a heavenly voice bade His disciples "Bear ye one another's burdens," but humanity has not yet risen to that point of self-sacrifice, and if ever so willing, how few the burdens are that one soul can bear for another. In the highways of Palestine; in prayer and fasting on the solitary mountain top; in the Garden of Gethsemane; before the judgment seat of Pilate; betrayed by one of His trusted disciples at His last supper; in His agonies on the cross, even Jesus of Nazareth, in these last sad days on earth, felt the awful solitude of self. Deserted by man, in agony he cries, "My God! My God! why hast Thou forsaken me?" And so it ever must be in the conflicting scenes of life, in the long weary march, each one walks alone. We may have many friends, love, kindness, sympathy and charity to smooth our pathway in everyday life, but in the tragedies and triumphs of human experience each mortal stands alone.

But when all artificial trammels are removed, and women are recognized as individuals, responsible for their own environments, thoroughly educated for all the positions in life they may be called to fill; with all the resources in themselves that liberal thought and broad culture can give; guided by their own conscience and judgment; trained to self-protection by a healthy development of the muscular system and skill in the use of weapons of defense, and stimulated to self-support by the knowledge of the business world and the pleasure that pecuniary independence must ever give; when women are trained in this way they will, in a measure, be fitted for those hours of solitude that come alike to all, whether prepared or otherwise. As in our extremity we must depend on ourselves, the dictates of wisdom point to complete individual development.

In talking of education how shallow the argument that each class must be educated for the special work it proposes to do, and all those faculties not needed in this special walk must lie dormant and utterly wither for want of use, when, perhaps, these will be very faculties needed in life's greatest emergencies. Some say, "Where is the use of drilling girls in the languages, the sciences, in law, medicine, theology?" As wives, mothers, housekeepers, cooks, they need a different curriculum from boys who are to fill all positions. The chief cooks in our great hotels and ocean steamers are men. In large cities men run the bakeries; they make our bread, cake and pies. They manage the laundries; they are now considered our best milliners and dressmakers. Because some men fill these departments of usefulness, shall we regulate the curriculum in Harvard and Yale to their present necessities? If not, why this talk in our best colleges of a curriculum for girls who are crowding into the trades and professions; teachers in all our public schools, rapidly filling many lucrative and honorable positions in life? They are showing, too, their calmness and courage in the most trying hours of human experience.

You have probably all read in the daily papers of the terrible storm in the Bay of Biscay when a tidal wave made such havoc on the shore, wrecking vessels, unroofing houses and carrying destruction everywhere. Among other buildings the woman's prison was demolished. Those who escaped saw men struggling to reach the shore. They promptly by clasping hands made a chain of themselves and pushed out into the sea, again and again, at the risk of their lives until they had brought six men to shore, carried them to a shelter, and did all in their power for their comfort and protection.

What special school of training could have prepared these women for this sublime moment of their lives. In times like this humanity rises above all college curriculum and recognizes Nature as the greatest of all teachers in the hour of danger and death. Women are already the equals of men in the whole realm of thought, in art, science, literature, and government. With telescopic vision they explore the starry firmament, and bring back the history of the planetary world. With chart and compass they pilot ships across the mighty deep, and with skillful finger send electric messages around the globe. In galleries of art the beauties of nature and the virtues of humanity are immortalized by them on their canvas and by their inspired touch dull blocks of marble are transformed into angles of light.

In music they speak again the language of Mendelssohn, Beethoven, Chopin, Schumann, and are worthy interpreters of their great thoughts. The poetry and novels of the century are theirs, and they have touched the keynote of reform in religion, politics, and social life. They fill the editor's and professor's chair and plead at the bar of justice, walk the wards of the hospital, and speak from the pulpit and the platform; such is the type of womanhood that an enlightened public sentiment welcomes today, and such the triumph of the facts of life over the false theories of the past.

Is it, then, consistent to hold the developed woman of this day within the same narrow political limits as the dame with the spinning wheel and knitting needle occupied in the past? No! no! Machinery has taken the labors of woman as well as man on its tireless shoulders; the loom and the spinning wheel are but dreams of the past; the pen, the brush, the easel, the chisel, have taken their places, while the hopes and ambitions of women are essentially changed.

We see reason sufficient in the outer conditions of human beings for individual liberty and development, but when we consider the self-dependence of every human soul we see the need of courage, judgment, and the exercise of every faculty of mind and body, strengthened and developed by use, in woman as well as man.

Whatever may be said of man's protecting power in ordinary conditions, mid all the terrible disasters by land and sea, in the supreme moments of danger, alone, woman must ever meet the horrors of the situation; the Angel of Death even makes no royal pathway for her. Man's love and sympathy enter only into the sunshine of our lives. In that solemn solitude of self, that links us with the immeasurable and the eternal, each soul lives alone forever. A recent writer says:

> I remember once, in crossing the Atlantic, to have gone upon the deck of the ship in midnight, when a dense black cloud enveloped the sky, and the great deep was roaring madly under the lashes of demoniac winds. My feeling was not of danger or fear (which is a base surrender of the immortal soul), but of utter desolation and loneliness; a little speck of life shut in by a tremendous darkness. Again I remember to have climbed the slopes of the Swiss Alps, up beyond the point where vegetation ceases, and the stunted conifers no longer struggle against the unfeeling blasts. Around me lay a huge confusion of rocks, out of which the gigantic ice peaks shot into the measureless blue of the heavens, and again my only feeling was the awful solitude.

> And yet, there is a solitude, which each and every one of us has always carried with him, more inaccessible than the ice-cold mountains, more profound than the midnight sea; the solitude of self. Our inner being, which we call ourself, no eye nor touch of man or angel has ever pierced. It is more hidden than the caves of the gnome; the sacred adytum of the oracle; the hidden chamber of eleusinian mystery, for to it only omniscience is permitted to enter.

Such is individual life. Who, I ask you, can take, dare take, on himself the rights, the duties, the responsibilities of another human soul?

Ida Wells-Barnett

(1862–1931)

SOUTHERN HORROR: LYNCH LAW IN ALL ITS PHASES
October 5, 1892

Ida Wells-Barnett was born Ida B. Wells in Holly Springs, Mississippi, mere months before the signing of the Emancipation Proclamation. Known mostly as an outspoken anti-lynching advocate, Wells contributed greatly to the causes of African-American and women's rights throughout her lauded career as an activist. In the following speech, delivered in New York City on October 5, 1892, Ida Wells-Barnett lectures on the atrocities of nineteenth-century lynching in the American South.

THE OFFENSE:

Wednesday evening May 24th, 1892, the city of Memphis was filled with excitement. Editorials in the daily papers of that date caused a meeting to be held in the Cotton Exchange Building; a committee was sent for the editors of the "Free Speech" an Afro-American journal published in that city, and the only reason the open threats of lynching that were made were not carried out because they could not be found. The cause of all this commotion was the following editorial published in the "Free Speech" May 21st, 1892, the Saturday previous.

"Eight negroes lynched since last issue of the 'Free Speech' one at Little Rock, Ark., last Saturday morning where the citizens broke (?) into the penitentiary and got their man; three near Anniston, Ala., one near New Orleans; and three at Clarksville, Ga., the last three for killing a white man, and five on the same old racket—the new alarm about raping white women. The same programme of hanging, then shooting bullets into the lifeless bodies was carried out to the letter.

Nobody in this section of the country believes the old thread bare lie that Negro men rape white women. If Southern white men are not careful, they will over-reach themselves and public sentiment will have a reaction; a conclusion will then be reached which will be very damaging to the moral reputation of their women."

"The Daily Commercial" of Wednesday following, May 25th, contained the following leader:

"Those negroes who are attempting to make the lynching of individuals of their race a means for arousing the worst passions of their kind are playing with a dangerous sentiment. The negroes may as well understand that there is no mercy for the negro rapist and little patience with his defenders. A negro organ printed in this city, in a recent issue publishes the following atrocious paragraph: 'Nobody in this section of the country believes the old thread-bare lie that negro men rape white women. If Southern white men are not careful they will over-reach themselves, and public sentiment will have a reaction; and a conclusion will be reached which will be very damaging to the moral reputation of their women.'

The fact that a black scoundrel is allowed to live and utter such loathsome and repulsive calumnies is a volume of evidence as to the wonderful patience of Southern whites. But we have had enough of it.

There are some things that the Southern white man will not tolerate, and the obscene intimations of the foregoing have brought the writer to the very outermost limit of public patience. We hope we have said enough."

The "Evening Scimitar" of same date, copied the "Commercial's" editorial with these words of comment: "Patience under such circumstances is not a virtue. If the negroes themselves do not apply the remedy without delay it will be the duty of those whom he has attacked to tie the wretch who utters these calumnies to a stake at the intersection of Main and Madison Sts., brand him in the forehead with a hot iron and perform upon him a surgical operation with a pair of tailor's shears."

Acting upon this advice, the leading citizens met in the Cotton Exchange Building the same evening, and threats of lynching were freely indulged, not by the lawless element upon which the deviltry of the South is usually saddled—but by the leading business men, in their leading business centre. Mr. Fleming, the business manager and owning a half interest in the Free Speech, had to leave town to escape the mob, and was afterwards ordered not to return; letters and telegrams sent me in New York where I was spending my vacation advised me that bodily harm awaited my return. Creditors took possession of the office and sold the outfit, and the "Free Speech" was as if it had never been.

The editorial in question was prompted by the many inhuman and fiendish lynchings of Afro-Americans which have recently taken place and was meant as a warning. Eight lynched in one week and five of them charged with rape! The thinking public will not easily believe freedom and education more brutalizing than slavery, and the world knows that the crime of rape was unknown during four years of civil war, when the white women of the South were at the mercy of the race which is all at once charged with being a bestial one.

Since my business has been destroyed and I am an exile from home because of that editorial, the issue has been forced, and as the writer of it I feel that the race and the public generally should have a statement of the facts as they exist. They will serve at the same time as a defense for the Afro-Americans Sampsons who suffer themselves to be betrayed by white Delilahs.

The whites of Montgomery, Ala., knew J. C. Duke sounded the keynote of the situation—which they would gladly hide from the world, when he said in his paper, "The Herald," five years ago: "Why is it that white women attract negro men now more than in former days? There was a time when such a thing was unheard of. There is a secret to this thing, and we greatly suspect it is the growing appreciation of white Juliets for colored Romeos." Mr. Duke, like the "Free Speech" proprietors, was forced to leave the city for reflecting on the "honah" of white women and his paper suppressed; but the truth remains that Afro-American men do not always rape (?) white women without their consent.

Mr. Duke, before leaving Montgomery, signed a card disclaiming any intention of slandering Southern white women. The editor of the "Free Speech" has no disclaimer to enter, but asserts instead that there are many white women in the South who would marry colored men if such an act would not place them at once beyond the pale of society and within the clutches of the law. The miscegnation laws of the South only operate against the legitimate union of the races; they leave the white man free to seduce all the colored girls he can, but it is death to the colored man who yields to the force and advances of a similar attraction in white women. White men lynch the offending Afro-American, not because he is a despoiler of virtue, but because he succumbs to the smiles of white women.

THE BLACK AND WHITE OF IT

The "Cleveland Gazette" of January 16, 1892, publishes a case in point. Mrs. J. S. Underwood, the wife of a minister of Elyria, Ohio, accused an Afro-American of rape. She told her husband that during his absence in 1888, stumping the State for the Prohibition Party, the man came to the kitchen door, forced his way in the house and insulted her. She tried to drive him out with a heavy poker, but he overpowered and chloroformed her, and when she revived her clothing was torn and she was in a horrible condition. She did not know the man but could identify him. She pointed out William Offett, a married man, who was arrested and, being in Ohio, was granted a trial.

The prisoner vehemently denied the charge of rape, but confessed he went to Mrs. Underwood's residence at her invitation and was criminally intimate with her at her request. This availed him nothing against the sworn testimony of a minister's wife, a lady of the highest respectability. He was found guilty, and entered the penitentiary, December 14, 1888, for fifteen years. Some time afterwards the woman's remorse led her to confess to her husband that the man was innocent.

These are her words: "I met Offett at the Post Office. It was raining. He was polite to me, and as I had several bundles in my arms he offered to carry them home for me, which he did. He had a strange fascination for me, and I invited him to call on me. He called, bringing chestnuts and candy for the children. By this means we got them to leave us alone in the room. Then I sat on his lap. He made a proposal to me and I readily consented. Why I did so, I do not know, but that I did is true. He visited me several times after that and each time I was indiscreet. I did not care after the first time. In fact I could not have resisted, and had no desire to resist."

When asked by her husband why she told him she had been outraged, she said: "I had several reasons for telling you. One was the neighbors saw the fellow here, another was, I was afraid I had contracted a loathsome disease, and still another was that I feared I might give birth to a Negro baby. I hoped to save my reputation by telling you a deliberate lie." Her husband horrified by the confession had Offett, who had already served four years, released and secured a divorce.

There are thousands of such cases throughout the South, with the difference that the Southern white men in insatiate fury wreak their vengeance without intervention of law upon the Afro-Americans who consort with their women. A few instances to substantiate the assertion that some white women love the company of the Afro-American will not be out of place. Most of these cases were reported by the daily papers of the South.

In the winter of 1885–6 the wife of a practicing physician in Memphis, in good social standing whose name has escaped me, left home, husband and children, and ran away with her black coachman. She was with him a month before her husband found and brought her home. The coachman could not be found. The doctor moved his family away from Memphis, and is living in another city under an assumed name.

In the same city last year a white girl in the dusk of evening screamed at the approach of some parties that a Negro had assaulted her on the street. He was captured, tried by a white judge and jury, that acquitted him of the charge. It is needless to add if there had been a scrap of evidence on which to convict him of so grave a charge he would have been convicted.

Sarah Clark of Memphis loved a black man and lived openly with him. When she was indicted last spring for miscegenration, she swore in court that she was *not* a white woman. This she did to escape the penitentiary and continued her illicit relation undisturbed. That she is of the lower class of whites, does not disturb the fact that she is a white woman. "The leading citizens" of Memphis are defending the "honor" of *all* white women, *demi-monde* included.

Since the manager of the "Free Speech" has been run away from Memphis by the guardians of the honor of Southern white women, a young girl living on Poplar St., who was discovered in intimate relations with a handsome mulatto young colored man, Will Morgan by name, stole her father's money to send the young fellow away from that father's wrath. She has since joined him in Chicago.

The Memphis "Ledger" for June 8th has the following: "If Lillie Bailey, a rather pretty white girl seventeen years of age, who is now at the City Hospital, would be somewhat less reserved about her disgrace there would be some very nauseating details in the story of her life. She is the mother of a little coon. The truth might reveal fearful depravity or it might reveal the evidence of a rank outrage. She will not divulge the name of the man who has left such black evidence of her disgrace, and, in fact, says it is a matter in which there can be no interest to the outside world. She came to Memphis nearly three months ago and was taken in at the Woman's Refuge in the southern part of the city. She remained there until a few weeks ago, when the child was born. The ladies in charge of the Refuge were horrified. The girl was at once sent to the City Hospital, where she has been since May 30th. She is a country girl. She came to Memphis from her father's farm, a short distance from Hernando, Miss. Just when she left there she would not say. In fact she says she came to Memphis from Arkansas, and says her home is in that State. She is rather good looking, has blue eyes, a low forehead and dark red hair. The ladies at the Woman's Refuge do not know anything about the girl further than what they learned when she was an inmate of the institution; and she would not tell much. When the child was born an attempt was made to get the girl to reveal the name of the Negro who had disgraced her, she obstinately refused and it was impossible to elicit any information from her on the subject."

Note the wording. "The truth might reveal fearful depravity or rank outrage." If it had been a white child or Lillie Bailey had told a pitiful story of Negro outrage, it would have been a case of woman's weakness or assault and she could have remained at the Woman's Refuge. But a Negro child and to withhold its father's name and thus prevent the killing of another Negro "rapist." A case of "fearful depravity."

The very week the "leading citizens" of Memphis were making a spectacle of themselves in defense of all white women of every kind, an Afro-American, M. Stricklin, was found in a white woman's room in that city. Although she made no outcry of rape, he was jailed and would have been lynched, but the woman stated she bought curtains of him (he was a furniture dealer) and his business in her room that night was to put them up. A white woman's word was taken as absolutely in this case as when the cry of rape is made, and he was freed.

What is true of Memphis is true of the entire South. The daily papers last year reported a farmer's wife in Alabama had given birth to a Negro child. When the Negro farm hand who was plowing in the field heard it he took the mule from the plow and fled. The dispatches also told of a woman in South Carolina who gave birth to a Negro child and charged three men with being its father, *every one of whom has since disappeared*. In Tuscumbia, Ala., the colored boy who was lynched there last year for assaulting a white girl told her before his accusers that he had met her there in the woods often before.

Frank Weems of Chattanooga who was not lynched in May only because the prominent citizens became his body guard until the doors of the penitentiary closed on him, had letters in his pocket from the white woman in the case, making the appointment with him. Edward Coy who was burned alive in Texarkana, January 1, 1892, died protesting his innocence. Investigation since as given by the Bystander in the Chicago Inter-Ocean, October 1, proves:

"1. The woman who was paraded as a victim of violence was of bad character; her husband was a drunkard and a gambler.

2. She was publicly reported and generally known to have been criminally intimate with Coy for more than a year previous.

3. She was compelled by threats, if not by violence, to make the charge against the victim.

4. When she came to apply the match Coy asked her if she would burn him after they had 'been sweethearting' so long.

5. A large majority of the 'superior' white men prominent in the affair are the reputed fathers of mulatto children.

These are not pleasant facts, but they are illustrative of the vital phase of the so-called 'race question,' which should properly be designated an earnest inquiry as to the best methods by which religion, science, law and political power may be employed to excuse injustice, barbarity and crime done to a people because of race and color. There can be no possible belief that these people were inspired by any consuming zeal to vindicate God's law against miscegnationists of the most practical sort. The woman was a willing partner in the victim's guilt, and being of the 'superior' race must naturally have been more guilty."

In Natchez, Miss., Mrs. Marshall, one of the *creme de la creme* of the city, created a tremendous sensation several years ago. She has a black coachman who was married, and had been in her employ several years. During this time she gave birth to a child whose color was remarked, but traced to some brunette ancestor, and one of the fashionable dames of the city was its godmother. Mrs. Marshall's social position was unquestioned, and wealth showered every dainty on this child which was idolized with its brothers and sisters by its white papa. In course of time another child appeared on the scene, but it was unmistakably dark. All were alarmed, and "rush of blood, strangulation" were the conjectures, but the doctor, when asked the cause, grimly told them it was a Negro child. There was a family conclave, the coachman heard of it and leaving his own family went West, and has never returned. As soon as Mrs. Marshall was able to travel she was sent away in deep disgrace. Her husband died within the year of a broken heart.

Ebenezer Fowler, the wealthiest colored man in Issaquena County, Miss., was shot down on the street in Mayersville, January 30, 1885, just before dark by an armed body of white men who filled his body with bullets. They charged him with writing a note to a white woman of the place, which they intercepted and which proved there was an intimacy existing between them.

Hundreds of such cases might be cited, but enough have been given to prove the assertion that there are white women in the South who love the Afro-American's company even as there are white men notorious for their preference for Afro-American women.

There is hardly a town in the South which has not an instance of the kind which is well-known, and hence the assertion is reiterated that "nobody in the South believes the old thread bare lie that negro men rape white women." Hence there is a growing demand among Afro-Americans that the guilt or innocence of parties accused of rape be fully established. They know the men of the section of the country who refuse this are not so desirous of punishing rapists as they pretend. The utterances of the leading white men show that with them it is not the crime but the *class*. Bishop Fitzgerald has become apologist for lynchers of the rapists of *white* women only. Governor Tillman, of South Carolina, in the month of June, standing under the tree in Barnwell, S.C., on which eight Afro-Americans were hung last year, declared that he would lead a mob to lynch a *negro* who raped a *white* woman." So say the pulpits, officials and newspapers of the South. But when the victim is a colored woman it is different.

Last winter in Baltimore, Md., three white ruffians assaulted a Miss Camphor, a young Afro-American girl, while out walking with a young man of her own race. They held her escort and outraged the girl. It was a deed dastardly enough to arouse Southern blood, which gives its horror of rape as excuse for lawlessness, but she was an Afro American. The case went to the courts, an Afro-American lawyer defended the men and they were acquitted.

In Nashville, Tenn., there is a white man, Pat Hanifan, who outraged a little Afro-American girl, and, from the physical injuries received, she has been ruined for life. He was jailed for six months, discharged, and is now a detective in that city. In the same city, last May, a white man outraged an Afro-American girl in a drug store. He was arrested, and released on bail at the trial. It was rumored that five hundred Afro-Americans had organized to lynch him. Two hundred and fifty white citizens armed themselves with Winchesters and guarded him. A cannon was placed in front of his home, and the Buchanan Rifles (State Militia) ordered to the scene for his protection. The Afro-American mob did not materialize. Only two weeks before Eph. Grizzard, who had only been *charged* with rape upon a white woman, had been taken from the jail, with Governor Buchanan and the police and militia standing by, dragged through the streets in broad daylight, knives plunged into him at every step, and with every fiendish cruelty a frenzied mob could devise, he was at last swung out on the bridge with hands cut to pieces as he tried to climb up the stanchions. A naked, bloody example of the blood-thristiness of the nineteenth century civilization of the Athens of the South! No cannon or military was called out in his defense. He dared to visit a white woman.

At the very moment these civilized whites were announcing their determination "to protect their wives and daughters," by murdering Grizzard, a white man was in the same jail for raping eight-year-old Maggie Reese, an Afro-American girl. He was not harmed. The "honor" of grown women who were glad enough to be supported by the Grizzard boys and Ed Coy, as long as the liaison was not

known, needed protection; they were white. The outrage upon helpless childhood needed no avenging in this case; she was black.

A white man in Guthrie, Oklahoma Territory, two months ago
inflicted such injuries upon another Afro-American child that she
died. He was not punished, but an attempt was made in the same
town in the month of June to lynch an Afro-American who visited a
white woman.

In Memphis, Tenn., in the month of June, Ellerton L. Dorr, who
is the husband of Russell Hancock's widow, was arrested for attempted rape on Mattie Cole, a neighbor's cook; he was only prevented from accomplishing his purpose, by the appearance of Mattie's
employer. Dorr's friends say he was drunk and not responsible for his
actions. The grand jury refused to indict him and he was discharged.

THE NEW CRY

The appeal of Southern whites to Northern sympathy and sanction, the adroit, insidious plea made by Bishop Fitzgerald for suspen-
sion of judgment because those "who condemn lynching express no
sympathy for the *white* woman in the case," falls to the ground in the
light of the foregoing.

From this exposition of the race issue in lynch law, the whole matter is explained by the well-known opposition growing out of slavery
to the progress of the race. This is crystalized in the oft-repeated slogan: "This is a white man's country and the white man must rule."
The South resented giving the Afro-American his freedom, the ballot
box and the Civil Rights Law. The raids of the Ku-Klux and White
Liners to subvert reconstruction government, the Hamburg and
Ellerton, S. C., the Copiah County Miss., and the Layfayette Parish,
La., massacres were excused as the natural resentment of intelligence
against government by ignorance.

Honest white men practically conceded the necessity of intelligence murdering ignorance to correct the mistake of the general
government, and the race was left to the tender mercies of the solid
South. Thoughtful Afro-Americans with the strong arm of the government withdrawn and with the hope to stop such wholesale massacres urged the race to sacrifice its political rights for sake of peace.
They honestly believed the race should fit itself for government, and
when that should be done, the objection to race participation in
politics would be removed.

But the sacrifice did not remove the trouble, nor move the South
to justice. One by one the Southern States have legally (?) disfran-
chised the Afro-American, and since the repeal of the Civil Rights
Bill nearly every Southern State has passed separate car laws with a

penalty against their infringement. The race regardless of advancement is penned into filthy, stifling partitions cut off from smoking cars. All this while, although the political cause has been removed, the butcheries of black men at Barnwell, S. C., Carrolton, Miss., Waycross, Ga., and Memphis, Tenn., have gone on; also the flaying alive of a man in Kentucky, the burning of one in Arkansas, the hanging of a fifteen year old girl in Louisiana, a woman in Jackson, Tenn., and one in Hollendale, Miss., until the dark and bloody record of the South shows 728 Afro-Americans lynched during the past 8 years. Not 50 of these were for political causes; the rest were for all manner of accusations from that of rape of white women, to the case of the boy Will Lewis who was hanged at Tullahoma, Tenn., last year for being drunk and "sassy" to white folks.

These statistics compiled by the Chicago "Tribune" were given the first of this year (1892). Since then, not less than one hundred and fifty have been known to have met violent death at the hands of cruel bloodthirsty mobs during the past nine months.

To palliate this record (which grows worse as the Afro-American becomes intelligent) and excuse some of the most heinous crimes that ever stained the history of a country, the South is shielding itself behind the plausible screen of defending the honor of its women. This, too, in the face of the fact that only *one-third* of the 728 victims to mobs have been *charged* with rape, to say nothing of those of that one-third who were innocent of the charge. A white correspondent of the Baltimore Sun declares that the Afro-American who was lynched in Chestertown, Md., in May for assault on a white girl was innocent; that the deed was done by a white man who had since disappeared. The girl herself maintained that her assailant was a white man. When that poor Afro-American was murdered, the whites excused their refusal of a trial on the ground that they wished to spare the white girl the mortification of having to testify in court.

This cry has had its effect. It has closed the heart, stifled the conscience, warped the judgment and hushed the voice of press and pulpit on the subject of lynch law throughout this "land of liberty." Men who stand high in the esteem of the public for christian character, for moral and physical courage, for devotion to the principles of equal and exact justice to all, and for great sagacity, stand as cowards who fear to open their mouths before this great outrage. They do not see that by their tacit encouragement, their silent acquiescence, the black shadow of lawlessness in the form of lynch law is spreading its wings over the whole country.

Men who, like Governor Tillman, start the ball of lynch law rolling for a certain crime, are powerless to stop it when drunken or criminal white toughs feel like hanging an Afro-American on any pretext.

Even to the better class of Afro-Americans the crime of rape is so revolting they have too often taken the white man's word and given lynch law neither the investigation for condemnation it deserved.

They forget that a concession of the right to lynch a man for a certain crime, not only concedes the right to lynch any person for any crime, but (so frequently is the cry of rape now raised) it is in a fair way to stamp us a race of rapists and desperadoes. They have gone on hoping and believing that general education and financial strength would solve the difficulty, and are devoting their energies to the accumulation of both.

The mob spirit has grown with the increasing intelligence of the Afro-American. It has left the out-of-the-way places where ignorance prevails, has thrown off the mask and with this new cry stalks in broad daylight in large cities, the centres of civilization, and is encouraged by the "leading citizens" and the press.

The Malicious and Untruthful White Press

The "Daily Commercial" and "Evening Scimitar" of Memphis, Tenn., are owned by leading business men of that city, and yet, in spite of the fact that there had been no white woman in Memphis outraged by an Afro-American, and that Memphis possessed a thrifty law-abiding, property owning class of Afro-Americans the "Commercial" of May 17th, under the head of "More Rapes, More Lynchings" gave utterance to the following:

"The lynching of three Negro scoundrels reported in our dispatches from Anniston, Ala., for a brutal outrage committed upon a white woman will be a text for much comment on 'Southern barbarism' by Northern newspapers; but we fancy it will hardly prove effective for campaign purposes among intelligent people. The frequency of these lynchings calls attention to the frequency of the crimes which causes lynching. The 'Southern barbarism' which deserves the serious attention of all people North and South, is the barbarism which preys upon weak and defenseless women. Nothing but the most prompt, speedy and extreme punishment can hold in check the horrible and bestial propensities of the Negro race. There is a strange similarity about a number of cases of this character which have lately occurred.

In each case the crime was deliberately planned and perpetrated by several Negroes. They watched for an opportunity when the women were left without a protector. It was not a sudden yielding to a fit of passion, but the consummation of a devilish purpose which has been seeking and waiting for the opportunity. This feature of the crime not only makes it the most fiendishly brutal, but it adds to the terror of the situation in the thinly settled country communities. No man can leave his family at night without the dread that some roving Negro ruffian is watching and waiting for this opportunity. The swift punishment which invariably follows these horrible crimes doubtless acts as a deterring effect upon the Negroes in that immediate neighborhood for a short time. But the lesson is not widely learned nor long remembered. Then such crimes, equally atrocious, have happened in quick succession, one in Tennessee, one in Arkansas, and one in Alabama. The facts of the crime appear to appeal more to the Negro's lustful imagination than the facts of the punishment do to his fears. He sets aside all fear of death in any form when opportunity is found for the gratification of his bestial desires.

There is small reason to hope for any change for the better. The commission of this crime grows more frequent every year. The generation of Negroes which have grown up since the war have lost in large measure the traditional and wholesome awe of the white race which kept the Negroes in subjection, even when their masters were in the army, and their families left unprotected except by the slaves themselves. There is no longer a restraint upon the brute passion of the Negro.

What is to be done? The crime of rape is always horrible, but for the Southern man there is nothing which so fills the soul with horror, loathing and fury as the outraging of a white woman by a Negro. It is the race question in the ugliest, vilest, most dangerous aspect. The Negro as a political factor can be controlled. But neither laws nor lynchings can subdue his lusts. Sooner or later it will force a crisis. We do not know in what form it will come."

In its issue of June 4th, the Memphis "Evening Scimitar" gives the following excuse for lynch law:

"Aside from the violation of white women by Negroes, which is the outcropping of a bestial perversion of instinct, the chief cause of trouble between the races in the South is the Negro's lack of manners. In the state of slavery he learned politeness from association with white people, who took pains to teach him. Since the emancipation came and the tie of mutual interest and regard between master and servant was broken, the Negro has drifted away into a state which is neither freedom nor bondage. Lacking the proper inspiration of the one and the restraining force of the other he has taken up the idea that boorish insolence is independence, and the exercise of a decent degree of breeding toward white people is identical with servile submission. In consequence of the prevalence of this notion there are

many Negroes who use every opportunity to make themselves offensive, particularly when they think it can be done with impunity.

We have had too many instances right here in Memphis to doubt
this, and our experience is not exceptional. *The white people won't
stand this sort of thing, and whether they be insulted as individuals or as a
race, the response will be prompt and effectual.* The bloody riot of 1866,
in which so many Negroes perished, was brought on principally by
the outrageous conduct of the blacks toward the whites on the streets.
It is also a remarkable and discouraging fact that the majority of such
scoundrels are Negroes who have received educational advantages at
the hands of the white taxpayers. They have got just enough of learning to make them realize how hopelessly their race is behind the other
in everything that makes a great people, and they attempt to 'get
even' by insolence, which is ever the resentment of inferiors. There
are well-bred Negroes among us, and it is truly unfortunate that they
should have to pay, even in part, the penalty of the offenses committed by the baser sort, but this is the way of the world. The innocent
must suffer for the guilty. If the Negroes as a people possessed a hun-
dredth part of the self-respect which is evidenced by the courteous
bearing of some that the 'Scimitar' could name, the friction between
the races would be reduced to a minimum. It will not do to beg the
question by pleading that many white men are also stirring up strife.
The Caucasian blackguard simply obeys the promptings of a depraved
disposition, and he is seldom deliberately rough or offensive toward
strangers or unprotected women.

The Negro tough, on the contrary, is given to just that kind of
offending, and he almost invariably singles out white people as his
victims."

On March 9th, 1892, there were lynched in this same city three of
the best specimens of young since-the-war Afro-American manhood.
They were peaceful, law-abiding citizens and energetic business men.

They believed the problem was to be solved by eschewing politics
and putting money in the purse. They owned a flourishing grocery
business in a thickly populated suburb of Memphis, and a white man
named Barrett had one on the opposite corner. After a personal difficulty which Barrett sought by going into the "People's Grocery"
drawing a pistol and was thrashed by Calvin McDowell, he (Barrett)
threatened to "clean them out." These men were a mile beyond the
city limits and police protection; hearing that Barrett's crowd was
coming to attack them Saturday night, they mustered forces and prepared to defend themselves against the attack.

When Barrett came he led a *posse* of officers, twelve in number,
who afterward claimed to be hunting a man for whom they had a

warrant. That twelve men in citizen's clothes should think it necessary to go in the night to hunt one man who had never before been
arrested, or made any record as a criminal has never been explained.
When they entered the back door the young men thought the threatened attack was on, and fired into them. Three of the officers were
wounded, and when the *defending* party found it was officers of the
law upon whom they had fired, they ceased and got away.

Thirty-one men were arrested and thrown in jail as "conspirators,"
although they all declared more than once they did not know they
were firing on officers. Excitement was at fever heat until the morning
papers, two days after, announced that the wounded deputy sheriffs
were out of danger. This hindered rather than helped the plans of the
whites. There was no law on the statute books which would execute
an Afro-American for wounding a white man, but the "unwritten
law" did. Three of these men, the president, the manager and clerk of
the grocery—"the leaders of the conspiracy"—were secretly taken
from jail and lynched in a shockingly brutal manner. "The Negroes are
getting too independent," they say, "we must teach them a lesson."

What lesson? The lesson of subordination. "Kill the leaders and it
will cow the Negro who dares to shoot a white man, even in self-
defense."

Although the race was wild over the outrage, the mockery of law
and justice which disarmed men and locked them up in jails where
they could be easily and safely reached by the mob—the Afro-
American ministers, newspapers and leaders counselled obedience to
the law which did not protect them.

Their counsel was heeded and not a hand was uplifted to resent the
outrage; following the advice of the "Free Speech," people left the
city in great numbers.

The dailies and associated press reports heralded these men to the
country as "toughs," and "Negro desperadoes who kept a low dive."
This same press service printed that the Negro who was lynched at
Indianola, Miss., in May, had outraged the sheriff's eight-year-old
daughter. The girl was more than eighteen years old, and was found
by her father in this man's room, who was a servant on the place.

Not content with misrepresenting the race, the mob-spirit was not
to be satisfied until the paper which was doing all it could to coun-
teract this impression was silenced. The colored people were resent-
ing their bad treatment in a way to make itself felt, yet gave the mob
no excuse for further murder, until the appearance of the editorial
which is construed as a reflection on the "honor" of the Southern
white women. It is not half so libelous as that of the "Commercial"
which appeared four days before, and which has been given in this

speech. They would have lynched the manager of the "Free Speech" for exercising the right of free speech if they had found him as quickly as they would have hung a rapist, and glad of the excuse to do so. The owners were ordered not to return, "The Free Speech" was suspended with as little compunction as the business of the "People's Grocery" broken up and the proprietors murdered.

THE SOUTH'S POSITION

Henry W. Grady in his well-remembered speeches in New England and New York pictured the Afro-American as incapable of self-government. Through him and other leading men the cry of the South to the country has been "Hands off! Leave us to solve our problem." To the Afro-American the South says, "the white man must and will rule." There is little difference between the Antebellum South and the New South.

Here white citizens are wedded to any method however revolting, any measure however extreme, for the subjugation of the young manhood of the race. They have cheated him out of his ballot, deprived him of civil rights or redress therefor in the civil courts, robbed him of the fruits of his labor, and are still murdering, burning and lynching him.

The result is a growing disregard of human life. Lynch law has spread its insidious influence till men in New York State, Pennsylvania and on the free Western plains feel they can take the law in their own hands with impunity, especially where an Afro-American is concerned. The South is brutalized to a degree not realized by its own inhabitants, and the very foundation of government, law and order, are imperilled.

Public sentiment has had a slight "reaction" though not sufficient to stop the crusade of lawlessness and lynching. The spirit of christianity of the great M. E. Church was aroused to the frequent and revolting crimes against a weak people, enough to pass strong condemnatory resolutions at its General Conference in Omaha last May. The spirit of justice of the grand old party asserted itself sufficiently to secure a denunciation of the wrongs, and a feeble declaration of the belief in human rights in the Republican platform at Minneapolis, June 7th. Some of the great dailies and weeklies have swung into line declaring that lynch law must go. The President of the United States issued a proclamation that it be not tolerated in the territories over which he has jurisdiction. Governor Northern and Chief Justice Bleckley of Georgia have proclaimed against it. The citizens of Chattanooga, Tenn., have set a worthy example in that they not only condemn lynch law, but her public men demanded a trial for Weems, the accused rapist, and guarded him while the trial was in progress. The trial only lasted ten minutes, and Weems chose to plead guilty and accept twenty-one years sentence, than invite the certain death which awaited him outside that cordon of police if he had told the truth and shown the letters he had from the white woman in the case.

Col. A. S. Colyar, of Nashville, Tenn., is so overcome with the horrible state of affairs that he addressed the following earnest letter to the Nashville "American." "Nothing since I have been a reading man has so impressed me with the decay of manhood among the people of Tennessee as the dastardly submission to the mob reign. We have reached the unprecedented low level; the awful criminal depravity of substituting the mob for the court and jury, of giving up the jail keys to the mob whenever they are demanded. We do it in the largest cities and in the country towns; we do it in midday; we do it after full, not to say formal, notice, and so thoroughly and generally is it acquiesced in that the murderers have discarded the formula of masks. They go into the town where everybody knows them, sometimes under the gaze of the governor, in the presence of the courts, in the presence of the sheriff and his deputies, in the presence of the entire police force, take out the prisoner, take his life, often with fiendish glee, and often with acts of cruelty and barbarism which impress the reader with a degeneracy rapidly approaching savage life. That the State is disgraced but faintly expresses the humiliation which has settled upon the once proud people of Tennessee. The State, in its majesty, through its organized life, for which the people pay liberally, makes but one record, but one note, and that a criminal falsehood, 'was hung by persons to the jury unknown.' The murder at Shelbyville is only a verification of what every intelligent man knew would come, because with a mob a rumor is as good as a proof."

These efforts brought forth apologies and a short halt, but the lynching mania was raged again through the past three months with unabated fury.

The strong arm of the law must be brought to bear upon lynchers in severe punishment, but this cannot and will not be done unless a healthy public sentiment demands and sustains such action.

The men and women in the South who disapprove of lynching and remain silent on the perpetration of such outrages, are particeps criminis, accomplices, accessories before and after the fact, equally guilty with the actual law-breakers who would not persist if they did not know that neither the law nor militia would be employed against them.

SELF HELP

In the creation of this healthier public sentiment, the Afro-American can do for himself what no one else can do for him. The world looks on with wonder that we have conceded so much and remain law-abiding under such great outrage and provocation.

To Northern capital and Afro-American labor the South owes its rehabilitation. If labor is withdrawn capital will not remain. The Afro-American is thus the backbone of the South. A thorough knowledge and judicious exercise of this power in lynching localities could many times effect a bloodless revolution. The white man's dollar is his god and to stop this will be to stop outrages in many localities.

The Afro-Americans of Memphis denounced the lynching of three of their best citizens, and urged and waited for the authorities to act in the matter and bring the lynchers to justice. No attempt was made to do so, and the black men left the city by thousands, bringing about great stagnation in every branch of business. Those who remained so injured the business of the street car company by staying off the cars, that the superintendent, manager and treasurer called personally on the editor of the "Free Speech," asked them to urge our people to give them their patronage again. Other business men became alarmed over the situation and the "Free Speech" was run away that the colored people might be more easily controlled. A meeting of white citizens in June, three months after the lynching, passed resolutions for the first time, condemning it. *But they did not punish the lynchers.* Every one of them was known by name, because they had been selected to do the dirty work, by some of the very citizens who passed these resolutions. Memphis is fast losing her black population, who proclaim as they go that there is no protection for the life and property of any Afro-American citizen in Memphis who is not a slave.

The Afro-American citizens of Kentucky, whose intellectual and financial improvement has been phenomenal, have never had a separate car law until now. Delegations and petitions poured into the Legislature against it, yet the bill passed and the Jim Crow Car of Kentucky is a legalized institution. Will the great mass of Negroes continue to patronize the railroad? A special from Covington, Ky., says:

"Covington, June 13th.—The railroads of the State are beginning to feel very markedly, the effects of the separate coach bill recently passed by the Legislature. No class of people in the State have so many and so largely attended excursions as the blacks. All these have been abandoned, and regular travel is reduced to a minimum. A competent authority says the loss to the various roads will reach $1,000,000 this year."

A call to a State Conference in Lexington, Ky., last June had delegates from every county in the State. Those delegates, the ministers, teachers, heads of secret and other orders, and the head of every family should pass the word around for every member of the race in Kentucky to stay off railroads unless obliged to ride. If they did so, and their advice was followed persistently the convention would not need to petition the Legislature to repeal the law or raise money to file a suit. The railroad corporations would be so effected they would in self-defense lobby to have the separate car law repealed. On the other hand, as long as the railroads can get Afro-American excursions they will always have plenty of money to fight all the suits brought against them. They will be aided in so doing by the same partisan public sentiment which passed the law. White men passed the law, and white judges and juries would pass upon the suits against the law, and render judgment in line with their prejudices and in deference to the greater financial power.

The appeal to the white man's pocket has ever been more effectual than all the appeals ever made to his conscience. Nothing, absolutely nothing, is to be gained by a further sacrifice of manhood and self-respect. By the right exercise of his power as the industrial factor of the South, the Afro-American can demand and secure his rights, the punishment of lynchers, and a fair trial for accused rapists.

Of the many inhuman outrages of this present year, the only case where the proposed lynching did *not* occur, was where the men armed themselves in Jacksonville, Fla., and Paducah, Ky., and prevented it. The only times an Afro-American who was assaulted got away has been when he had a gun and used it in self-defense.

The lesson this teaches and which every Afro-American should ponder well, is that a Winchester rifle should have a place of honor in every black home, and it should be used for that protection which the law refuses to give. When the white man who is always the aggressor knows he runs as great risk of biting the dust every time his Afro-American victim does, he will have greater respect for Afro-American life. The more the Afro-American yields and cringes and begs, the more he has to do so, the more he is insulted, outraged and lynched.

The assertion has been substantiated throughout that the press contains unreliable and doctored reports of lynchings, and one of the most necessary things for the race to do is to get these facts before the public. The people must know before they can act, and there is no educator to compare with the press.

The Afro-American papers are the only ones which will print the truth, and they lack means to employ agents and detectives to get at the facts. The race must rally a mighty host to the support of their journals, and thus enable them to do much in the way of investigation.

A lynching occurred at Port Jarvis, N.Y., the first week in June. A white and colored man were implicated in the assault upon a white girl. It was charged that the white man paid the colored boy to make the assault, which he did on the public highway in broad day time, and was lynched. This, too was done by "parties unknown." The white man in the case still lives. He was imprisoned and promises to fight the case on trial. At the preliminary examination, it developed that he had been a suitor of the girl's. She had repulsed and refused him, yet had given him money, and he had sent threatening letters demanding more.

The day before this examination she was so wrought up, she left home and wandered miles away. When found she said she did so because she was afraid of the man's testimony. Why should she be afraid of the prisoner? Why should she yield to his demands for money if not to prevent him exposing something he knew? It seems explainable only on the hypothesis that a *liaison* existed between the colored boy and the girl, and the white man knew it. The press is singularly silent. Has it a motive? We owe it to ourselves to find out.

The story comes from Larned, Kansas, Oct. 1st, that a young white lady held at bay until daylight, without alarming any one in the house, "a burly Negro" who entered her room and bed. The "burly Negro" was promptly lynched without investigation or examination of inconsistent stories.

A house was found burned down near Montgomery, Ala., in Monroe County, Oct. 13th, a few weeks ago; also the burned bodies of the owners and melted piles of gold and silver.

These discoveries led to the conclusion that the awful crime was not prompted by motives of robbery. The suggestion of the whites was that "brutal lust was the incentive, and as there are nearly 200 Negroes living within a radius of five miles of the place the conclusion was inevitable that some of them were the perpetrators."

Upon this "suggestion" probably made by the real criminal, the mob acted upon the "conclusion" and arrested ten Afro-Americans, four of whom, they tell the world, confessed to the deed of murdering Richard L. Johnson and outraging his daughter, Jeanette. These four men, Berrell Jones, Moses Johnson, Jim and John Packer, none of them 25 years of age, upon this conclusion, were taken from jail, hanged, shot, and burned while yet alive the night of Oct. 12th. The same report says Mr. Johnson was on the best of terms with his Negro tenants.

The race thus outraged must find out the facts of this awful hurling of men into eternity on supposition, and give them to the indifferent and apathetic country. We feel this to be a garbled report, but how can we prove it?

Near Vicksburg, Miss., a murder was committed by a gang of burglars. Of course it must have been done by Negroes, and Negroes were arrested for it. It is believed that 2 men, Smith Tooley and John Adams belonged to a gang controlled by white men and, fearing exposure, on the night of July 4th, they were hanged in the Court House yard by those interested in silencing them. Robberies since committed in the same vicinity have been known to be by white men who had their faces blackened. We strongly believe in the innocence of these murdered men, but we have no proof. No other news goes out to the world save that which stamps us as a race of cutthroats, robbers and lustful wild beasts. So great is Southern hate and prejudice, they legally (?) hung poor little thirteen year old Mildrey Brown at Columbia, S.C., Oct. 7th, on the circumstantial evidence that she poisoned a white infant. If her guilt had been proven unmistakably, had she been white, Mildrey Brown would never have been hung.

The country would have been aroused and South Carolina disgraced forever for such a crime. The Afro-American himself did not know as he should have known as his journals should be in a position to have him know and act.

Nothing is more definitely settled than he must act for himself. I have shown how he may employ the boycott, emigration and the press, and I feel that by a combination of all these agencies can be effectually stamped out lynch law, that last relic of barbarism and slavery. "The gods help those who help themselves."

Lucy Stone

(1818–1893)

THE PROGRESS OF FIFTY YEARS
May 15, 1893

Lucy Stone, a prominent nineteenth-century abolitionist and suffragette, became the first woman to receive a college degree in Massachusetts when she graduated from Oberlin College in 1847. In addition to being the wife of famed abolitionist Henry Brown Blackwell and mother of the important human rights leader Alice Stone Blackwell, Stone is perhaps best remembered as the first woman ever recorded in the United States to keep her own last name after marriage. The following was the last speech that Stone would ever make, delivered to the Congress of Women at World's Fair in Chicago mere months before her death in 1893.

THE COMMENCEMENT of the last fifty years is about the beginning of that great change and improvement in the condition of women which exceeds all the gains of hundreds of years before.

Four years in advance of the last fifty, in 1833, Oberlin College, in Ohio, was founded. Its charter declared its grand object, "To give the most useful education at the least expense of health, time, and money, and to extend the benefits of such education to both sexes and to all classes; and the elevation of the female character by bringing within the reach of the misjudged and neglected sex all the instructive privileges which have hitherto unreasonably distinguished the leading sex from theirs." These were the words of Father Shippen, which, if not heard in form, were heard in fact as widely as the world. The opening of Oberlin to women marked an epoch. In all outward circumstances this beginning was like the coming of the Babe of Bethlehem—in utter poverty. Its first hall was of rough slabs with the bark on still. Other departments corresponded. But a new Messiah had come.

Get but a truth once uttered, and 'tis like
A star new born that drops into its place;
And which, once circling in its placid round,
Not all the tumult of the earth can shake.

Henceforth the leaves of the tree of knowledge were for women, and for the healing of the nations. About this time Mary Lyon began a movement to establish Mt. Holyoke Seminary. Amherst College was near by. Its students were educated to be missionaries. They must have educated wives. It was tacitly understood and openly asserted that Mt. Holyoke Seminary was to meet this demand. But, whatever the reason, the idea was born that women could and should be educated. It lifted a mountain load from woman. It shattered the idea, everywhere pervasive as the atmosphere, that women were incapable of education, and would be less womanly, less desirable in every way, if they had it. However much it may have been resented, women accepted the idea of their intellectual inequality. I asked my brother: "Can girls learn Greek?"

The anti-slavery cause had come to break stronger fetters than those that held the slave. The idea of equal rights was in the air. The wail of the slave, his clanking fetters, his utter need, appealed to everybody. Women heard. Angelina and Sarah Grimke and Abby Kelly went out to speak for the slaves. Such a thing had never been heard of. An earthquake shock could hardly have startled the community more. Some of the abolitionists forgot the slave in their efforts to silence the women. The Anti-Slavery Society rent itself in twain over the subject. The Church was moved to its very foundation in opposition. The Association of Congregational Churches issued a "Pastoral Letter" against the public speaking of women. The press, many-tongued, surpassed itself in reproaches upon these women who had so far departed from their sphere as to speak in public. But, with anointed lips and a consecration which put even life itself at stake, these peerless women pursued the even tenor of their way, saying to their opponents only: "Woe is me if I preach not this gospel of freedom for the slave." Over all came the melody of Whittier's:

"When woman's heart is breaking
Shall woman's voice be hushed?"

I think, with never-ending gratitude, that the young women of today do not and can never know at what price their right to free speech and to speak at all in public has been earned. Abby Kelly once entered a church only to find herself the subject of the sermon, which was preached from the text: "This Jezebel is come among us also." They jeered at her as she went along the street. They threw stones at her. They pelted her with bad eggs as she stood on the platform. Some of the advocates of the very cause for which she endured all this were ready to drive her from the field. Mr. Garrison and Wendell Phillips stood by her. But so great was the opposition that one faction of the abolitionists left and formed a new organization, after a vain effort to put Abby Kelly off from the committee to which she had been nominated.

The right to education and to free speech having been gained for woman, in the long run every other good thing was sure to be obtained.

Half a century ago women were at an infinite disadvantage in regard to their occupations. The idea that their sphere was at home, and only at home, was like a band of steel on society. But the spinning-wheel and the loom, which had given employment to women, had been superseded by machinery, and something else had to take their places. The taking care of the house and children, and the family sewing, and teaching the little summer school at a dollar per week, could not supply the needs nor fill the aspirations of women. But every departure from these conceded things was met with the cry, "You want to get out of your sphere," or, "To take women out of their sphere;" and that was to fly in the face of Providence, to unsex yourself—in short, to be monstrous women, women who, while they orated in public, wanted men to rock the cradle and wash the dishes. We pleaded that whatever was fit to be done at all might with propriety be done by anybody who did it well; that the tools belonged to those who could use them; that the possession of a power presupposed a right to its use. This was urged from city to city, from state to state. Women were encouraged to try new occupations. We endeavored to create that wholesome discontent in women that would compel them to reach out after far better things. But every new step was a trial and a conflict. Men printers left when women took the type. They formed unions and pledged themselves not to work for men who employed women. But these tools belonged to women, and today a great army of women are printers unquestioned.

When Harriet Hosmer found within herself the artist soul, and sought by the study of anatomy to prepare herself for her work, she was repelled as out of her sphere, and indelicate, and not a medical college in all New England or in the Middle States would admit her. She persevered, aided by her father's wealth and influence. Dr. McDowell, the dean of the medical college in St. Louis, admitted her. The field of art is now open to women, but as late as the time when models for the statue of Charles Sumner were made, although that of Annie Whitney, in the judgment of the committee, took precedence of all the rest, they refused to award her the contract for the statue when they knew that the model was the work of a woman. But her beautiful Samuel Adams and Lief Ericsson, and the fine handiwork of other artists, are argument and proof that the field of art belongs to women.

When Mrs. Tyndall, of Philadelphia, assumed her husband's business after his death, importing chinaware, sending her ships to China, enlarging her warehouses and increasing her business, the fact was quoted as a wonder. When Mrs. Young, of Lowell, Mass., opened a shoe-store in Lowell, though she sold only shoes for women and children, people peered curiously in to see how she looked. Today the whole field of trade is open to woman.

When Elizabeth Blackwell studied medicine and put up her sign in New York, she was regarded as fair game, and was called a "she doctor." The college that had admitted her closed its doors afterward against other women, and supposed they were shut out forever. But Dr. Blackwell was a woman of fine intellect, of great personal worth and a level head. How good it was that such a woman was the first doctor! She was well equipped by study at home and abroad, and prepared to contend with prejudice and every opposing thing. Dr. Zakrzewska was with her, and Dr. Emily Blackwell soon joined them. At a price the younger women doctors do not know, the way was opened for women physicians.

The first woman minister, Antoinette Brown, had to meet ridicule and opposition that can hardly be conceived to-day. Now there are women ministers, east and west, all over the country.

In Massachusetts, where properly qualified "persons" were allowed to practice law, the Supreme Court decided that a woman was not a "person," and a special act of the legislature had to be passed before Miss Lelia Robinson could be admitted to the bar. But today women are lawyers.

Fifty years ago the legal injustice imposed upon women was appalling. Wives, widows and mothers seemed to have been hunted out by the law on purpose to see in how many ways they could be wronged and made helpless. A wife by her marriage lost all right to any personal property she might have. The income of her land went to her husband, so that she was made absolutely penniless. If a woman earned a dollar by scrubbing, her husband had a right to take the dollar and go and get drunk with it and beat her afterwards. It was his dollar. If a woman wrote a book the copyright of the same belonged to her husband and not to her. The law counted out in many states how many cups and saucers, spoons and knives and chairs a widow might have when her husband died. I have seen many a widow who took the cups she had bought before she was married and bought them again after her husband died, so as to have them legally. The law gave no right to a married woman to any legal existence at all. Her legal existence was suspended during marriage. She could neither sue nor be sued. If she had a child born alive the law gave her husband the use of all her real estate as long as he should live, and called it by the pleasant name of "the estate by courtesy." When the husband died the law gave the widow the use of one-third of the real estate belonging to him, and it was called the "widow's encumbrance." While the law dealt thus with her in regard to her property, it dealt still more hardly with her in regard to her children. No married mother could have any right to her child, and in most of the states of the Union that is the law to-day. But the laws in regard to the personal and property rights of women have been greatly changed and improved, and we are very grateful to the men who have done it.

We have not only gained in the fact that the laws are modified. Women have acquired a certain amount of political power. We have now in twenty states school suffrage for women. Forty years ago there was but one. Kentucky allowed widows with children of school age to vote on school questions. We have also municipal suffrage for women in Kansas, and full suffrage in Wyoming, a state larger than all New England.

The last half century has gained for women the right to the highest education and entrance to all professions and occupations, or nearly all. As a result we have women's clubs, the Woman's Congress, women's educational and industrial unions, the moral education societies, the Woman's Relief Corps, police matrons, the Woman'sChristian Temperance Union, colleges for women, and co-educational colleges and the Harvard Annex, medical schools and medical societies open to women, women's hospitals, women in the pulpit, women as a power in the press, authors, women artists, women's beneficent societies and Helping Hand societies, women school supervisors, and factory inspectors and prison inspectors, women on state boards of charity, the International Council of Women, the Woman's National Council, and last, but not least, the Board of Lady Managers. And not one of these things was allowed women fifty years ago, except the opening at Oberlin. By what toil and fatigue and patience and strife and the beautiful law of growth has all this been wrought? These things have not come of themselves. They could not have occurred except as the great movement for women has brought them out and about. They are part of the eternal order, and they have come to stay. Now all we need is to continue to speak the truth fearlessly, and we shall add to our number those who will turn the scale to the side of equal and full justice in all things.

Jane Addams

(1860–1935)

A MODERN LEAR
1896

Jane Addams was one of the nation's foremost advocates for social justice, pacifism, universal suffrage, and women's rights. In 1889, Addams joined with Ellen Gates Starr to found Hull House, one of the nation's first and most well-known settlement houses, before going on to become the first woman president of the National Conference of Charities and Correction, the first head of the National Federation of Settlements, and the first vice president of the National American Suffrage Association. In 1931, Addams was awarded the Nobel Peace prize in recognition of her years of antiwar advocacy. The following speech was delivered both at the Chicago Women's Club and the Twentieth Century Club of Boston in 1896, and later published as a magazine article in 1912.

THOSE OF US who lived in Chicago during the summer of 1894 were confronted by a drama which epitomized and, at the same time, challenged the code of social ethics under which we live, for a quick series of unusual events had dispelled the good nature which in happier times envelopes the ugliness of the industrial situation. It sometimes seems as if the shocking experiences of that summer, the barbaric instinct to kill, roused on both sides, the sharp division into class lines, with the resultant distrust and bitterness, can only be endured if we learn from it all a great ethical lesson. To endure is all we can hope for. It is impossible to justify such a course of rage and riot in a civilized community to whom the methods of conciliation and control were open. Every public-spirited citizen in Chicago during that summer felt the stress and perplexity of the situation and asked himself, "How far am I responsible for this social disorder? What can be done to prevent such outrageous manifestations of ill-will?"

If the responsibility of tolerance lies with those of the widest vision, it behooves us to consider this great social disaster, not alone in its legal aspect nor in its sociological bearings, but from those deep human motives, which, after all, determine events.

During the discussions which followed the Pullman strike, the defenders of the situation were broadly divided between the people pleading for individual benevolence and those insisting upon social righteousness; between those who held that the philanthropy of the president of the Pullman company had been most ungratefully received and those who maintained that the situation was the inevitable outcome of the social consciousness developing among working people.

In the midst of these discussions the writer found her mind dwelling upon a comparison which modified and softened all her judgments. Her attention was caught by the similarity of ingratitude suffered by an indulgent employer and an indulgent parent. King Lear came often to her mind. We have all shared the family relationship and our code of ethics concerning it is somewhat settled. We also bear a part in the industrial relationship, but our ethics concerning that are still uncertain. A comparative study of these two relationships presents an advantage, in that it enables us to consider the situation from the known experience toward the unknown. The minds of all of us reach back to our early struggles, as we emerged from the state of self-willed childhood to a recognition of the family claim.

We have all had glimpses of what it might be to blaspheme against family ties; to ignore the elemental claim they make upon us, but on the whole we have recognized them, and it does not occur to us to throw them over. The industrial claim is so difficult; the ties are so intangible that we are constantly ignoring them and shirking the duties which they impose. It will probably be easier to treat of the tragedy of the Pullman strike as if it were already long past when we compare it to the family tragedy of Lear which has already become historic to our minds and which we discuss without personal feeling.

Historically considered, the relation of Lear to his children was archaic and barbaric, holding in it merely the beginnings of a family life, since developed. We may in later years learn to look back upon the industrial relationships in which we are now placed as quite as incomprehensible and selfish, quite as barbaric and undeveloped, as was the family relationship between Lear and his daughters. We may then take the relationship of this unusually generous employer at Pullman to his own townful of employees as at least a fair one, because so exceptionally liberal in many of its aspects. King Lear doubtless held the same notion of a father's duty that was held by the other fathers of his time; but he alone was a king and had kingdoms to bestow upon his children. He was unique, therefore, in the magnitude of his indulgence, and in the magnitude of the disaster which followed it. The sense of duty held by the president of the Pullman company doubtless represents the ideal in the minds of the best of the present employers as to their obligations toward their employees, but he projected this ideal more magnificently than the others. He alone gave his men so model a town, such perfect surroundings. The magnitude of his indulgence and failure corresponded and we are forced to challenge the ideal itself: the same ideal which, more or less clearly defined, is floating in the minds of all philanthropic employers.

This older tragedy implied maladjustment between individuals; the forces of the tragedy were personal and passionate. This modern tragedy in its inception is a maladjustment between two large bodies of men, an employing company and a mass of employees. It deals not with personal relationships, but with industrial relationships.

Owing, however, to the unusual part played in it by the will of one man, we find that it closely approaches Lear in motif. The relation of the British King to his family is very like the relation of the president of the Pullman company to his town; the denouement of a daughter's break with her father suggests the break of the employees with their benefactor. If we call one an example of the domestic tragedy, the other of the industrial tragedy, it is possible to make them illuminate each other.

It is easy to discover striking points of similarity in the tragedies of the royal father and the philanthropic president of the Pullman company. The like quality of ingratitude they both suffered is at once apparent. It may be said that the ingratitude which Lear received was poignant and bitter to him in proportion as he recalled the extraordinary benefits he had heaped upon his daughters, and that he found his fate harder to bear because he had so far exceeded the measure of a father's duty, as he himself says. What, then, would be the bitterness of a man who had heaped extraordinary benefits upon those toward whom he had no duty recognized by common consent; who had not only exceeded the righteousness of the employer, but who had worked out original and striking methods for lavishing goodness and generosity? More than that, the president had been almost persecuted for this goodness by the more utilitarian members of his company and had at one time imperilled his business reputation for the sake of the benefactions to his town, and he had thus reached the height of sacrifice for it. This model town embodied not only his hopes and ambitions, but stood for the peculiar effort which a man makes for that which is misunderstood.

It is easy to see that although the heart of Lear was cut by ingratitude and by misfortune, it was cut deepest of all by the public pity of his people, in that they should remember him no longer as a king and benefactor, but as a defeated man who had blundered through oversoftness. So the heart of the Chicago man was cut by the unparalleled publicity which brought him to the minds of thousands as a type of oppression and injustice, and to many others as an example of the evil of an irregulated sympathy for the "lower classes." He who had been dined and feted throughout Europe as the creator of a model town, as the friend and benefactor of workingmen, was now execrated by workingmen throughout the entire country. He had not only been good to those who were now basely ungrateful to him, but he felt himself deserted by the admiration of his people.

In shops such as those at Pullman, indeed, in all manufacturing affairs since the industrial revolution, industry is organized into a vast social operation. The shops are managed, however, not for the development of the workman thus socialized, but for the interests of the company owning the capital. The divergence between the social form and the individual aim becomes greater as the employees are more highly socialized and dependent, just as the clash in a family is more vital in proportion to the development and closeness of the family tie. The president of the Pullman company went further than the usual employer does. He socialized not only the factory but the form in which his workmen were living. He built and, in a great measure, regulated an entire town. This again might have worked out into a successful associated effort, if he had had in view the sole good of the inhabitants thus socialized, if he had called upon them for self-expression and had made the town a growth and manifestation of their wants and needs, But, unfortunately, the end to be obtained became ultimately commercial and not social, having in view the payment to the company of at least 4 per cent on the money invested, so that with this rigid requirement there could be no adaptation of rent to wages, much less to needs. The rents became statical and the wages competitive, shifting inevitably with the demands of trade. The president assumed that he himself knew the needs of his men, and so far from wishing them to express their needs he denied to them the simple rights of trade organization, which would have been, of course, the merest preliminary to an attempt at associated expression. If we may take the dictatorial relation of Lear to Cordelia as a typical and most dramatic example of the distinctively family tragedy, one will asserting its authority through all the entanglement of wounded affection, and insisting upon its selfish ends at all costs, may we not consider the absolute authority of this employer over his town as a typical and dramatic example of the industrial tragedy? One will directing the energies of many others, without regard to their desires, and having in view in the last analysis only commercial results?

It shocks our ideal of family life that a man should fail to know his daughter's heart because she awkwardly expressed her love, that he should refuse to comfort and advise her through all difference of opinion and clashing of will. That a man should be so absorbed in his own indignation as to fail to apprehend his child's thought; that he should lose his affection in his anger, is really no more unnatural than that the man who spent a million of dollars on a swamp to make it sanitary for his employees, should refuse to speak to them for ten minutes, whether they were in the right or wrong; or that a man who had given them his time and thought for twenty years should withdraw from them his guidance when he believed them misled by ill-advisers and wandering in a mental fog; or that he should grow hard and angry when they needed tenderness and help.

Lear ignored the common ancestry of Cordelia and himself. He forgot her royal inheritance of magnanimity, and also the power of obstinacy which he shared with her. So long had he thought of himself as the noble and indulgent father that he had lost the faculty by which he might perceive himself in the wrong. Even when his spirit was broken by the storm he declared himself more sinned against than sinning. He could believe any amount of kindness and goodness of himself, but could imagine no fidelity on the part of Cordelia unless she gave him the sign he demanded.

The president of the Pullman company doubtless began to build his town from an honest desire to give his employees the best surroundings. As it developed it became a source of pride and an exponent of power, that he cared most for when it gave him a glow of benevolence. Gradually, what the outside world thought of it became of importance to him and he ceased to measure its usefulness by the standard of the men's needs. The theater was complete in equipment and beautiful in design, but too costly for a troupe who depended upon the patronage of mechanics, as the church was too expensive to be rented continuously. We can imagine the founder of the town slowly darkening his glints of memory and forgetting the common stock of experience which he held with his men. He cultivated the great and noble impulses of the benefactor, until the power of attaining a simple human relationship with his employees, that of frank equality with them, was gone from him. He, too, lost the faculty of affectionate interpretation, and demanded a sign. He and his employees had no mutual interest in a common cause.

Was not the grotesque situation of the royal father and the philanthropic employer to perform so many good deeds that they lost the power of recognizing good in beneficiaries? Were not both so absorbed in carrying out a personal plan of improvement that they failed to catch the great moral lesson which their times offered them? This is the crucial point to the tragedies and may be further elucidated.

Lear had doubtless swung a bauble before Cordelia's baby eyes that he might have the pleasure of seeing the little pink and tender hands stretched for it. A few years later he had given jewels to the young princess, and felt an exquisite pleasure when she stood before him, delighted with her gaud and grateful to her father. He demanded the same kind of response for his gift of the kingdom, but the gratitude must be larger and more carefully expressed, as befitted such a gift. At the opening of the drama he sat upon his throne ready for this enjoyment, but instead of delight and gratitude he found the first dawn of character. His daughter made the awkward attempt of an untrained soul to be honest, to be scrupulous in the expressions of its feelings. It was new to him that his child should be moved by a principle outside of himself, which even his imagination could not follow; that she had caught the notion of an existence so vast that her relationship as a daughter was but part of it.

Perhaps her suitors, the King of France or the Duke of Burgundy, had first hinted to the young Cordelia that there was a fuller life beyond the seas. Certain it is that someone had shaken her from the quiet measure of her insular existence and that she had at last felt the thrill of the world's life. She was transformed by a dignity which recast her speech and made it self-contained, as is becoming a citizen of the world. She found herself in the sweep of a notion of justice so large that the immediate loss of a kingdom seemed of little consequence to her. Even an act which might be construed as disrespect to her father was justified in her eyes because she was vainly striving to fill out this larger conception of duty.

The test which comes sooner or later to many parents had come to Lear, to maintain the tenderness of the relation between father and child, after that relation had become one between adults; to be contented with the responses which this adult made to the family claim, while, at the same time, she felt the tug upon her emotions and faculties of the larger life, the life which surrounds and completes the individual and family life, and which shares and widens her attention. He was not sufficiently wise to see that only that child can fulfill the family claim in its sweetness and strength who also fulfills the larger claim, that the adjustment of the lesser and larger implies no conflict. The mind of Lear was not big enough for this test. He failed to see anything but the personal slight involved; the ingratitude alone reached him. It was impossible for him to calmly watch his child developing beyond the strength of his own mind and sympathy.

Without pressing the analogy too hard may we not compare the indulgent relation of this employer to his town to the relation which existed between Lear and Cordelia? He fostered his employees for many years, gave them sanitary houses and beautiful parks, but in their extreme need, when they were struggling with the most difficult question which the times could present to them, when, if ever, they required the assistance of a trained mind and a comprehensive outlook, he lost his touch and had nothing wherewith to help them. He did not see the situation. He had been ignorant of their gropings toward justice. His conception of goodness for them had been cleanliness, decency of living, and above all, thrift and temperance. He had provided them means for all this; had gone further, and given them opportunities for enjoyment and comradeship. But he suddenly found his town in the sweep of a world-wide moral impulse. A movement had been going on about him and through the souls of his workingmen of which he had been unconscious. He had only heard of this movement by rumor. The men who consorted with him at his club and in his business had spoken but little of it, and when they had discussed it had contemptuously called it the "Labor Movement," headed by deadbeats and agitators. Of the force and power of this movement, of all the vitality within it, of that conception of duty which induces men to go without food and to see their wives and children suffer for the sake of securing better wages for fellow-workmen whom they have never seen, this president had dreamed absolutely nothing. But his town had at last become swept into this larger movement, so that the giving up of comfortable homes, of beautiful surroundings, seemed as naught to the men within its grasp.

Outside the ken of this philanthropist, the proletariat had learned to say in many languages that "the injury of one is the concern of all." Their watchwords were brotherhood, sacrifice, the subordination of individual and trade interests to the good of the working class; and their persistent strivings were toward the ultimate freedom of that class from the conditions under which they now labor.

Compared to these watchwords the old ones which the philanthropic employer had given his town were negative and inadequate.

When this movement finally swept in his own town, or, to speak more fairly, when in their distress and perplexity his own employees appealed to the organized manifestation of this movement, they were quite sure that simply because they were workmen in distress they would not be deserted by it. This loyalty on the part of a widely ramified and well organized union toward the workmen in a "scab shop," who had contributed nothing to its cause, was certainly a manifestation of moral power.

That the movement was ill-directed, that it was ill-timed and disastrous in results, that it stirred up and became confused in the minds of the public with the elements of riot and bloodshed, can never touch the fact that it started from an unselfish impulse.

In none of his utterances or correspondence did the president of the company for an instant recognize this touch of nobility, although one would imagine that he would gladly point out this bit of virtue, in what he must have considered the moral ruin about him. He stood throughout pleading for the individual virtues, those which had distinguished the model workman of his youth, those which had enabled him and so many of his contemporaries to rise in life, when "rising in life" was urged upon every promising boy as the goal of his efforts. Of the new code of ethics he had caught absolutely nothing. The morals he had taught his men did not fail them in their hour of confusion. They were self-controlled and destroyed no property. They were sober and exhibited no drunkenness, even though obliged to hold their meetings in the saloon hall of a neighboring town. They repaid their employer in kind, but he had given them no rule for the higher fellowship and life of association into which they were plunged.

The virtues of one generation are not sufficient for the next, any more than the accumulations of knowledge possessed by one age are adequate to the needs of another.

Of the virtues received from our fathers we can afford to lose none. We accept as a precious trust those principles and precepts which the race has worked out for its highest safeguard and protection. But merely to preserve those is not enough. A task is laid upon each generation to enlarge their application, to ennoble their conception, and, above all, to apply and adapt them to the peculiar problems presented to it for solution.

The president of this company desired that his employees should possess the individual and family virtues, but did nothing to cherish in them those social virtues which his own age demanded. He rather substituted for that sense of responsibility to the community, a feeling of gratitude to himself, who had provided them with public buildings, and had laid out for them a simulacrum of public life.

Is it strange that when the genuine feeling of the age struck his town this belated and almost feudal virtue of personal gratitude fell before it?

Day after day during that horrible suspense, when the wires constantly reported the same message, "The president of the company holds that there is nothing to arbitrate," one longed to find out what was in the mind of this man, to unfold his ultimate motive. One concludes that he must have been sustained by the consciousness of being in the right. Only that could have held him against the great desire for fair play which swept over the country. Only the training which an arbitrary will receives by years of consulting first its own personal and commercial ends could have made it strong enough to withstand the demands for social adjustment. He felt himself right from the commercial standpoint, and could not see the situation from the social standpoint. For years he had gradually accustomed himself to the thought that his motive was beyond reproach; that his attitude to his town was always righteous and philanthropic. Habit held him persistent in this view of the case through all the changing conditions.

The diffused and subtle notion of dignity held by the modern philanthropist bears a curious analogy to the personal barbaric notion of dignity held by Lear. The man who persistently paced the seashore, while the interior of his country was racked with a strife which he alone might have arbitrated, lived out within himself the tragedy of King Lear. The shock of disaster upon egotism is apt to produce self-pity. It is possible that his self-pity and loneliness may have been so great and absorbing as to completely shut out from his mind a compunction of derelict duty. He may have been unconscious that men were charging him with a shirking of the issue.

Lack of perception is the besetting danger of the egoist, from whatever cause his egoism arises and envelopes him. But, doubtless, philanthropists are more exposed to this danger than any other class of people within the community. Partly because their efforts are overestimated, as no standard of attainment has yet been established, and partly because they are the exponents of a large amount of altruistic feeling with which the community has become equipped and which has not yet found adequate expression, they are therefore easily idealized.

Long ago Hawthorne called our attention to the fact that philanthropy ruins, or is fearfully apt to ruin, the heart, "the rich juices of which God never meant should be pressed violently out, and distilled into alcoholic liquor by an unnatural process; but it should render life sweet, bland and gently beneficent."

One might add to this observation that the muscles of this same heart may be stretched and strained until they lose the rhythm of the common heartbeat of the rest of the world.

Modern philanthropists need to remind themselves of the old definition of greatness: that it consists in the possession of the largest share of the common human qualities and experiences, not in the acquirements of peculiarities and excessive virtues. Popular opinion calls him the greatest of Americans who gathered to himself the largest amount of American experience, and who never forgot when he was in Washington how the "crackers" in Kentucky and the pioneers of Illinois thought and felt, striving to retain their thoughts and feelings, and to embody only the mighty will of the "common people." The danger of professionally attaining to the power of the righteous man, of yielding to the ambition "for doing good," compared to which the ambitious for political position, learning, or wealth are vulgar and commonplace, ramifies throughout our modern life, and is a constant and settled danger of philanthropy.

In so far as philanthropists are cut off from the influence of the Zeit-Geist, from the code of ethics which rule the body of men, from the great moral life springing from our common experiences, so long as they are "good to people," rather than "with them," they are bound to accomplish a large amount of harm. They are outside of the influence of that great faith which perennially springs up in the hearts of the people, and re-creates the world.

In spite of the danger of overloading the tragedies with moral reflections, a point ought to be made on the other side. It is the weakness in the relation of the employees to the employer, the fatal lack of generosity in the attitude of workmen toward the company under whose exactions they feel themselves wronged.

In reading the tragedy of King Lear, Cordelia does not escape our censure. Her first words are cold, and we are shocked by her lack of tenderness. Why should she ignore her father's need for indulgence, and be so unwilling to give him what he so obviously craved? We see in the old king "the overmastering desire of being beloved, which is selfish, and yet characteristic of the selfishness of a loving and kindly nature alone." His eagerness produces in us a strange pity for him, and we are impatient that his youngest and best-beloved child cannot feel this, even in the midst of her search for truth and her newly acquired sense of a higher duty. It seems to us a narrow conception that would break thus abruptly with the past, and would assume that her father had no part in her new life. We want to remind her that "pity, memory and faithfulness are natural ties," and surely as much to be prized as is the development of her own soul. We do not admire the Cordelia "who loves according to her bond" as we later admire the same Cordelia who comes back from France that she may include in her happiness and freer life the father whom she had deserted through her self-absorption. She is aroused to her affection through her pity, but when the floodgates are once open she acknowledges all. It sometimes seems as if only hardship and sorrow could arouse our tenderness, whether in our personal or social relations; that the king, the prosperous man, was the last to receive the justice which can come only through affectionate interpretation. We feel less pity for Lear on his throne than in the storm, although he is the same man, bound up in the same self-righteousness, and exhibiting the same lack of self-control.

As the vision of the life of Europe caught the sight and quickened the pulses of Cordelia, so a vision of the wider life has caught the sight of workingmen. After the vision has once been seen it is impossible to do aught but to press toward its fulfillment. We have all seen it. We are all practically agreed that the social passion of the age is directed toward the emancipation of the wage-worker; that a great accumulation of moral force is overmastering men and making for this emancipation as in another time it has made for the emancipation of the slave; that nothing will satisfy the aroused conscience of men short of the complete participation of the working classes in the spiritual, intellectual and material inheritance of the human race. But just as Cordelia failed to include her father in the scope of her salvation and selfishly took it for herself alone, so workingmen in the dawn of the vision are inclined to claim it for themselves, putting out of their thoughts the old relationships; and just as surely as Cordelia's conscience developed in the new life and later drove her back to her father, where she perished, drawn into the cruelty and wrath which had now become objective and tragic, so the emancipation of working people will have to be inclusive of the employer from the first or it will encounter many failures, cruelties and reactions. It will result not in the position of the repentant Cordelia but in that of King Lear's two older daughters.

If the workingmen's narrow conception of emancipation was fully acted upon, they would hold much the same relationship to their expropriated employer that the two older daughters held to their abdicated father. When the kingdom was given to them they received it as altogether their own, and were dominated by a sense of possession; "it is ours not yours" was never absent from their consciousness. When Lear ruled the kingdom he had never been without this sense of possession, although he expressed it in indulgence and condescending kindness. His older daughters expressed it in cruelty, but the motive of father and children was not unlike. They did not wish to be reminded by the state and retinue of the old King that he had been the former possessor. Finally, his mere presence alone reminded them too much of that and they banished him from the palace. That a newly acquired sense of possession should result in the barbaric, the incredible scenes of bitterness and murder, which were King Lear's portion, is not without a reminder of the barbaric scenes in our political and industrial relationships, when the sense of possession, to obtain and to hold, is aroused on both sides. The scenes in Paris during the political revolution or the more familiar scenes at the mouths of the mines and the terminals of railways occur to all of us.

The doctrine of emancipation preached to the wage-workers alone runs an awful risk of being accepted for what it offers them, for the sake of fleshpots, rather than for the human affection and social justice which it involves. This doctrine must be strong enough in its fusing power to touch those who think they lose, as well as those who think they gain. Only thus can it become the doctrine of a universal movement.

The new claim on the part of the toiling multitude, the new sense of responsibility on the part of the well-to-do, arise in reality from the same source. They are in fact the same "social compunction," and, in spite of their widely varying manifestations, logically converge into the same movement. Mazzini once preached, "the consent of men and your own conscience are two wings given you whereby you may rise to God." It is so easy for the good and powerful to think that they can rise by following the dictates of conscience by pursuing their own ideals, leaving those ideals unconnected with the consent of their fellowmen. The president of the Pullman company thought out within his own mind a beautiful town. He had power with which to build this town, but he did not appeal to nor obtain the consent of the men who were living in it. The most unambitious reform, recognizing the necessity for this consent, makes for slow but sane and strenuous progress, while the most ambitious of social plans and experiments, ignoring this, is prone to the failure of the model town of Pullman.

The man who insists upon consent, who moves with the people, is bound to consult the feasible right as well as the absolute right. He is often obliged to attain only Mr. Lincoln's "best possible," and often have the sickening sense of compromising with his best convictions. He has to move along with those whom he rules toward a goal that neither he nor they see very clearly till they come to it. He has to discover what people really want, and then "provide the channels in which the growing moral force of their lives shall flow." What he does attain, however, is not the result of his individual striving, as a solitary mountain climber beyond the sight of the valley multitude, but it is underpinned and upheld by the sentiments and aspirations of many others. Progress has been slower perpendicularly, but incomparably greater because lateral.

He has not taught his contemporaries to climb mountains, but he has persuaded the villagers to move up a few feet higher. It is doubtful if personal ambition, whatever may have been its commercial results, has ever been of any value as a motive power in social reform.

But whatever it may have done in the past, it is certainly too archaic to accomplish anything now. Our thoughts, at least for this generation, cannot be too much directed from mutual relationships and responsibilities. They will be warped, unless we look all men in the face, as if a community of interests lay between, unless we hold the mind open, to take strength and cheer from a hundred connections.

To touch to vibrating response the noble fibre in each man, to pull these many fibres, fragile, impalpable and constantly breaking, as they are, into one impulse, to develop that mere impulse through its feeble and tentative stages into action, is no easy task, but lateral progress is impossible without it.

If only a few families of the English speaking race had profited by the dramatic failure of Lear, much heart-breaking and domestic friction might have been spared. Is it too much to hope that some of us will carefully consider this modern tragedy, if perchance it may contain a warning for the troublous times in which we live? By considering the dramatic failure of the liberal employer's plans for his employees we may possibly be spared useless industrial tragedies in the uncertain future which lies ahead of us.

Mary Harris "Mother" Jones

(1837*–1930)

APPEAL TO THE CAUSE OF MINERS
IN THE PAINT CREEK DISTRICT
August 15, 1912

Mary Harris "Mother" Jones was best known for her work as a union organizer and her skills as an eloquent orator. A founding member of the Industrial Workers of the World (also known as "Wobblies"), Jones was an active and influential part of numerous labor movements, most notably the United Mine Workers and the Socialist Party of America. Jones delivered this speech on the front steps of the State Capitol building in Charleston, West Virginia, on August 15, 1912.

THIS, MY FRIENDS, marks, in my estimation, the most remarkable move ever made in the State of West Virginia. It is a day that will mark history in the long ages to come. What is it? It is an uprising of the oppressed against the master class.

From this day on, my friends, Virginia—West Virginia—shall march in the front of the Nation's States. To me, I think, the proper thing to do is to read the purpose of our meeting here today—why these men have laid down their tools, why these men have come to the statehouse.

> To His Excellency William E. Glasscock,
> *Governor of the State of West Virginia:*
>
> It is respectfully represented unto your excellency that the owners of the various coal mines doing business along the valley of Cabin Creek, Kanawha County, W. Va., are maintaining and have at present in their employ a large force of armed guards, armed with Winchesters, a dan-

---

*Mother Jones herself claimed to have been born on May 1, 1830, though this is now widely held to be incorrect, and stated by her for the symbolic value of the date.

gerous and deadly weapon; also having in their possession three Gatlins guns, which they have stationed at commanding positions overlooking the Cabin Creek Valley, which said weapons said guards use for the purpose of browbeating, intimidating, and menacing the lives of all the citizens who live in said valley, who are not in accord with the management of the coal companies, which guards are cruel, and their conduct toward the citizens is such that it would be impossible to give a detailed account of.

Therefore suffice it to say, however, that they beat, abuse, maim, and hold up citizens without process of law; deny freedom of speech, a provision guaranteed by the Constitution; deny the citizens the right to assemble in a peaceable manner for the purpose of discussing questions in which they are concerned. Said guards also hold up a vast body of laboring men who live at the mines, and so conduct themselves that a great number of men, women, and children live in a state of constant fear, unrest, and dread.

We hold that the stationing of said guards along the public highways and public places is a menace to the general welfare of the State. That such action on the part of the companies in maintaining such guards is detrimental to the best interests of society and an outrage against the honor and dignity of the State of West Virginia. [Loud applause.]

As citizens interested in the public weal and general welfare, and believing that law and order and peace should ever abide, that the spirit of brotherly love and justice and freedom should everywhere exist, we must tender our petition that you would bring to bear all the powers of your office as chief executive of this State for the purpose of disarming said guards and restoring to the citizens of said valley all the rights guaranteed by the Constitution of the United States and said State.

In duty bound, in behalf of the miners of the State of West Virginia.

I want to say, with all due respect to the governor—I want to say to you that the governor will not, can not, do anything, for this reason: The governor was placed in this building by Scott and Elkins and he don't dare oppose them. [Loud applause.] Therefore you are asking the governor of the State to do something that he can not do without betraying the class he belongs to. [Loud applause.]

I remember the governor in a State, when Grover Cleveland was perched in the White House—Grover Cleveland said he would send the Federal troops out, and the governor of that State said, "Will you? If you do, I will meet your Federal troops with the State troops, and we will have it out." Old Grover never sent the troops; he took back water. [Applause and cries of "Yes; he did."]

You see, my friends, how quickly the governor sent his militia when the coal operators got scared to death. [Applause.]

I have no objection to the militia. I would always prefer the militia, but there was no need in this country for the militia; none whatever.

They were law-abiding people, and the women and children. They were held up on the highways, caught in their homes, and pulled out like rats and beaten up—some of them. I said, "If there is no one else in the State of West Virginia to protest, I will protest." [Loud applause, and cries of "Yes, she will: 'Mother' will."]

The womanhood of this State shall not be oppressed and beaten and abused by a lot of contemptible, damnable bloodhounds hired by the operators. They wouldn't keep their dog where they keep you fellows. You know that. They have a good place for their dogs and a slave to take care of them. The mine owners' wives will take the dogs up, and say, "I love you, dea-h" [trying to imitate by tone of voice].

My friends the day for petting dogs is gone; the day for raising children to a nobler manhood and better womanhood is here. [Applause and cries of "Amen! Amen!"]

You have suffered; I know you have suffered. I was with you nearly three years in this State. I went to jail; went to the Federal courts; but I never took any back water. I still unfurl the red flag of industrial freedom; no tyrant's face shall you know, and I call you today into that freedom—long perch on the bosom—[Interrupted by applause.]

I am back again to find you, my friends, in a state of industrial peonage—after 10 years' absence I find you in a state of industrial peonage.

The superintendent at Acme—I went up there, and they said we were unlawful—we had an unlawful mob along. Well, I will tell you the truth; we took a couple of guns because we knew we were going to meet some thugs, and by jimminy—[Interrupted by applause.]

We will prepare for the job, just like Lincoln and Washington did. We took lessons from them, and we are here to prepare for the job.

Well, when I came out on the public road the superintendent— you know the poor salary slave—he came out and told me that there were notaries public there and a squire—one had a peg leg—and the balance had pegs in their skulls. [Applause.]

They forbid me speaking on the highway, and said that if I didn't discontinue I would be arrested. Well, I want to tell you one thing, I don't run into jail, but when the bloodhounds undertake to put me in jail I will go there. I have gone there. I would have had the little peg-leg squire arrest me, only I knew this meeting was going to be pulled off to-day, to let the world know what was going on in West Virginia. When I get through with them, by the Eternal God, they will be glad to let me alone.

I am not afraid of jails. We build the jails, and when we get ready we will put them behind the bars. That may happen very soon; things happen overnight.

Now, brothers, not in all the history of the labor movement have I got such an inspiration as I have got from you here to-day. Your banners are history; they will go down to the future ages, to the children unborn, to tell them the slave has risen, children must be free.

The labor movement was not originated by man. The labor movement, my friends, was a command from God Almighty. He commanded the prophets thousands of years ago to go down and redeem the Israelites that were in bondage, and he organized the men into a union and went to work. And they said, "The masters have made us gather straw; they have been more cruel than they were before." "What are we going to do?" The prophet said, "A voice from heaven has come to get you together." They got together and the prophet led them out of the land of bondage and robbery and plunder into the land of freedom. And when the army of the pirates followed them the Dead Sea opened and swallowed them up, and for the first time the workers were free.

And so it is. That can well be applied to the State of West Virginia. When I left Cabin Creek 10 years ago to go to another terrific battle field every man on Cabin Creek was organized—every single miner. The mine owners and the miners were getting along harmoniously; they had an understanding and were carrying it out. But they had some traitors who made a deal with the mine owners and the organization was driven out of Cabin Creek. There were no better miners in the whole State of West Virginia than on Cabin Creek, and no better operators in those days. You got along together. They were trying to make it happy and comfortable for you, but the demon came and tore the organization to pieces and you are at war to-day.

I hope, my friends, that you and the mine owners will put aside the breach and get together before I leave the State. But I want to say, make no settlement until they sign up that every bloody murderer of a guard has got to go. [Loud applause.]

This is done, my friends, beneath the flag our fathers fought and bled for, and we don't intend to surrender our liberty. [Applause.]

I have a document issued 18 years ago telling how they must handle the labor movement—pat them on the back; make them believe that they were your devoted friends. I hold the document, taken from their statement in Washington. It plainly states, "We have got to crucify them, but we have got to do it cunningly." And they have been doing it cunningly. But I want to say, in answer to your statements, that you are dealing with a different class of workers to-day than 18 years ago. We have begun education; we have educated the workers and you can't enslave them. They will come again, and you will either take to the ocean and get out of the Nation and leave us alone or you will settle right with us. [Loud applause.]

It is different now, my friends. It was Mark Hanna who said some years ago—the shrewdest politician American ever had—he said, "I want to tell you that before 1912 the Republican and Democratic Parties will be about to get their deathblow."

Never in the history of the United States was there such an upheaval as there is to-day. The politicians are cutting each other's throats, eating each other up; they are for the offices. Teddy, the monkey chaser, had a meeting in Chicago. He was blowing his skull off his carcass about race suicide. God Almighty, bring him down the C. & O. and he will never say another word about race suicide. The whole population seems to be made up out of "kids." Every woman has three babies in her arms and nine on the floor. So you will see there is no danger of race suicide. When he sees this he will keep his mouth shut on that.

See the condition we are in today. There is a revolution. There is an editorial in one of the papers in your own State showing how little they have done for the workers, that the workers are awakening. The literature is being circulated among them. I myself have circulated millions and millions of pieces of literature in this country and awakened the miners. On the trains they say, "Oh, Mother, you gave us a book that woke us up." As long as you woke up right, it is all right. He says, "I have woke up right." Then, if you woke up right, you are my children.

O you men of wealth! O you preachers! You are going over to China and sending money over there for Jesus. For God's sake, keep it at home; we need it. Let me tell you, them fellows are owned body and soul by the ruling class and they would rather take a year in hell with Elkins than ninety-nine in heaven. [Loud applause.] Do you find a minister preaching against the guards?

[Cries from the audience: "They are traitors; moral cowards."]

He will preach about Jesus, but not about the guards.

When we were crossing the bridge at Washington the bloodhounds were at the company store. These bloodhounds might have thrown me into the river and I wouldn't have known it. The men were hollering "Police! Police!" I said, "What is the matter with you?" They said, "O God! Murder! Murder!" Another one came out, and his feet never touched the sidewalk.

My boys came running to me and said, "Oh, Mother, they are killing the boys." The traction car turned the corner. I said, "Call them boys here." Then they went; they thought I had an army with me. Then I picked up a boy streaming with blood where the hounds had beat him.

You are to blame. You have voted for the whole gang of commercial pirates every time you get a chance to free yourselves.

It is time to clean them up.

[Cries of "She is right; she is right!"]

If this Nation is to march onward and upward, the day of change is here.

I had been reading of the *Titanic* when she went down. Did you read of her? The big guns wanted to save themselves, and the fellows that were guiding below took up a club and said, "We will save our people." And then the papers came out and said those millionaires tried to save the women. O, Lord, why don't they give up their millions if they want to save the women and children? Why do they rob them of home; why do they rob millions of women to fill the hell holes of capitalism?

I realize—I remember what they did to me—the Guggenheims—I remember what the Guggenheim bloodhounds did to me one night in Colorado. They went to the hotel after we had organized the slaves. I took the 4 o'clock train for the southern fields, and the bloodhounds, the chief of police, and the whole gang of commercial bloodhounds came up to the hotel and went to the register to find my room, and the hotel keeper said that I had left at 4 o'clock. We had a meeting that night. They took a fellow and drove him down the street barefooted and put him on the train and told him never to come back. And we are very civilized! They don't do that in Russia; it is in America.

They took me and put me in jail—I had the smallpox—I had the Helen Gould smallpox covering me all over. And at 4 o'clock in the morning they came and the bloodhounds—Helen Gould's bloodhounds—and they bound 400 miners in Colorado for gold, and threw their widows and orphans out on the highways in the snow. When I was fighting a battle with those wretches they put me into a pen which you built, a pesthouse, it was burned down before morning, it wasn't worth 50 cents. We went down by a store, and the storekeeper said, "God Almighty, put us down in the cellar and they won't know us, put the dirty clothes on us—when them dirty clothes found out that there was such a lot of rotten carcasses under them, the dirty clothes turned over." [Applause and laughter.]

If your sheriff had done his duty as a citizen of this State and according to his oath, he would have disarmed the guards and then there would have been no more trouble.

[Cries of: "That is right, that is right."]

Just make me governor for one month. I won't ask for a sheriff or policeman, and I will do business, and there won't be a guard stay in the State of West Virginia. [Applause.] The mine owners won't take 69,000 pounds of coal in dockage off of you fellows. Sixty-nine thousand pounds of coal they docked you for, and a few pounds of slate, and then they give to Jesus on Sunday.

They give your missionary women a couple of hundred dollars and rob you under pretense of giving to Jesus. Jesus never sees a penny of it, and never heard of it. They use it for the women to get a jag on and then go and hollow for Jesus.

I wish I was God Almighty, I would throw down something some night from heaven and get rid of the whole blood-sucking bunch. [Laughter and applause.]

I want to show you here that the average wages you fellows get in this country is $500 a year. Before you get a thing to eat there is $20 taken out a month, which leaves about $24 a month.

Then you go to the "pluck-me" stores and want to get something to eat for your wife, and you are off that day, and the child comes back and says, "Papa, I can't get anything." "Why," he says, "There is $4 coming to me." The child says, "They said there was nothing coming to you." And the child goes back crying without a mouthful of anything to eat. The father goes to the "pluck-me" store and says to the manager, "There is $4 coming to me," and the manager says, "Oh, no; we have kept that for rent." "You charge $6 a month, and there are only three days gone." "Well," he says, "It is a rule that two-thirds of the rent is to be kept if there is only one day."

That is honesty. Do you wonder these women starve? Do you wonder at this uprising? And you fellows have stood it entirely too long. It is time now to put a stop to it. We will give the governor until to-morrow night to take them guards out of Cabin Creek.

[Very loud applause, and cries of: "And no longer."]

Here on the steps of the Capital of West Virginia, I say that if the governor won't make them go then we will make them go.

[Loud applause, and cries of "That we will," "Only one more day," "The guards have got to go."]

We have come to the chief executive, we have asked him, and he couldn't do anything. [Laughter.]

The prosecuting attorney is of the same type—another fellow belonging to the ruling class. [Applause and murmurings in the crowd.] Hush up there, hush up, hush up.

I want to tell you that the governor will get until to-morrow night,

Friday night, to get rid of his bloodhounds, and if they are not gone, we will get rid of them. [Loud applause.]

Aye men, aye men, inside of this building, aye women, come with me and see the horrible pictures, see the horrible condition the ruling class has put these women in. Aye, they destroy women. Look at those little children, the rising generation, yes, look at the little ones, yes, look at the women assaulted. Some one said that that place ought to be drained up there. The mine owner's home is drained; the superintendent's home is drained. But I want to ask you, when a man works 10 or 11 hours in the foul gas of the mine day after day, if he is in condition to come out and drain.

[Cries of "Not on your life; no."]

I have worked, boys, I have worked with you for years. I have seen the suffering children, and in order to be convinced I went into the mines on the night shift and day shift and helped the poor wretches to load coal at times. We lay down at noon and we took our lunches and we talked our wrongs over, we gathered together at night and asked "How will we remedy things?" We organized secretly, and after a while held public meetings. We got our people together in those organized States. To-day the mine owners and the miners come together. They meet each other and shake hands, and have no more war in those States, and the workingmen are becoming more intelligent. And I am one of those my friends, I don't care about your woman suffrage and the temperance brigade or any other of your class associations, I want women of the coming day to discuss and find out the cause of child crucifixion, that is what I want to find out.

I have worked in the factories of Georgia and Alabama, and these bloodhounds were tearing the hands off of children and working them 14 hours a day until I fought for them. They made them put up every Saturday money for missionary work in China. I know what I am talking about. I am not talking haphazard, I have the goods.

Go down, men of to-day, who rob and exploit, go down into hell and look at the ruins you have put there, look at the jails. We pay $6,000,000 a year to chain men like demons in a bastile—and we call ourselves civilized. Six million dollars a year we pay for jails, and nothing for education.

I have been in jail more than once, and I expect to go again. If you are too cowardly to fight, I will fight. You ought to be ashamed of yourselves, actually to the Lord you ought, just to see one old woman who is not afraid of all the bloodhounds. How scared those villains are when one woman 80 years old, with her head gray, can come in and scare hell out of the whole bunch. [Laughter.] We didn't scare them? The mine owners run down the street like a mad dog to-day. They ask who started this thing. I started it, I did it, and I am not afraid to tell you if you are here, and I will start more before I leave West Virginia. I started this mass meeting to-day, I had these banners written, and don't accuse anybody else of the job. [Loud applause.]

It is freedom or death, and your children will be free. We are not going to leave a slave class to the coming generation, and I want to say to you that the next generation will not charge us for what we have done; they will charge and condemn us for what we have left undone. [Cries of "That is right."]

You have got your bastile. Yes; we have no fears of them at all. I was put out at 12 o'clock at night—and landed with 5 cents in my pocket—by seven bayonets in the State of Colorado. The governor told me—he is a corporation rat, you know—he told me never to come back. A man is a fool, if he is a governor, to tell a woman not to do a thing. [Loud applause, and cries of "Tell them again; tell them about it."]

I went back next day and I have been back since the fight, and he hasn't bothered me. He has learned it won't do to tamper with women of the right metal. You have a few cats [mocking]—they are not women, they are what you call ladies. There is a difference between women and ladies. The modern parasites made ladies, but God Almighty made women. [Applause and cries of "Tell us one more."]

Now, my boys, you are mine; we have fought together, we have hungered together, we have marched together, but I can see victory in the Heavens for you. I can see the hand above you guiding and inspiring you to move onward and upward. No white flag—we can not raise it; we must not raise it. We must redeem the world.

Go into our factories, see how the conditions are there, see how women are ground up for the merciless money pirates, see how many of the poor wretches go to work with crippled bodies. I talked with a mother who had her small children working. She said to me, "Mother, they are not of age, but I had to say they were; I had to tell them they were of age so they could get a chance to help me to get something to eat." She said after they were there a little while, "I have saved $40, the first I ever saw. I put that into a cow and we had some milk for the little ones." In all the years her husband had put in the earth digging out wealth, he never got a glimpse of $40 until he had to take his infant boys, that ought to go to school, and sacrifice them.

If there was no other reason that should stimulate every man and woman to fight this damnable system of commercial pirates. [Cries of "Right, right."] That alone should do it, my friends.

Is there a committee here? I want to take a committee of the well-fed fellows and well-dressed fellows; I want to present this to the governor. Be very polite. Don't get on your knees. Get off your knees and stand up. None of these fellows are better than you, they are only flesh and blood—that is the truth.

(Committee formed around "Mother" and start into the capitol building.) These fellows all want to go and see the king. [Laughter.]

I will give the press a copy of this resolution and this petition, that was given to the governor.

Now, my boys, guard rule and tyranny will have to go; there must be an end. I am going up Cabin Creek. I am going to hold meetings there. I am going to claim the right of an American citizen. I was on this earth before these operators were. I was in this country before these operators. I have been 74 years under this flag. I have got the right to talk. I have seen its onward march. I have seen the growth of oppression, and I want to say to you, my friends, I am going to claim my right as a citizen of this Nation. I won't violate the law; I will not kill anybody or starve anybody; but I will talk unsparingly of all the corporation bloodhounds we can bring to jail. [Laughter.]

I have no apologies to offer. I have seen your children murdered; I have seen you blown to death in the mines, and there was no redress. A fellow in Colorado says, "Why don't you prop the mines?" The operator said, "Oh, hell; Dagoes are cheaper than props!" Every miner is a Dago with the blood-sucking pirates, and they are cheaper than props, because if they kill a hundred of you, well, it was your fault; there must be a mine inspector kept there.

The night before the little Johnson boys were killed the mine inspector—John Laing is a mine owner, he wouldn't inspect them—the mine inspector went there and said the mines are propped securely. The next morning the little Johnson children went to work, and when they were found their hands were clasped in their dinner buckets with two biscuits.

You work for Laing day after day. He is a mine inspector, but he wouldn't be if I had anything to say about it. He would take a back seat.

Boys, I want to say to you, obey the law. Let me say to the governor and let me say to the mine owners—let me say to all people—that I will guarantee there will be no destruction of property.

In the first place, that is our property. It is inside where our jobs are. We have every reason to protect it. In the mines is where our jobs are. We are not out to destroy property; we are out to preserve and protect property, and I will tell you why. We are going to get more wages and we are going to stop the docking system. Put that down. Your day for docking is done. Stop it. If they don't stop it, we will. [Cries of "Good!" "Good!"]

We'll take care of the property; there will be no property destroyed [Cries of "Not a bit!"]

Not a bit; and if you want your property protected these miners will protect it for you, and they won't need a gun. [Cries of "It is our interest to do so!"]

We will protect it at the risk of our lives. I know the miners; I have marched with 10,000—20,000—and destroyed no property. We had 20,000 miners in Pennsylvania, but destroyed no property.

They used to do that years ago, but after we have educated them they saw that violence was not the idea. We stopped it; we organized; we brought them to school once again. I will tell you why we are not going to destroy your property, Mr. Governor: Because one of these days we are going to take over the mines. [Loud applause.]

That is what we are going to do; we are going to take over those mines.

The Government has a mine in North Dakota. It works eight hours—not a minute more. There are no guards, no police, no militia. The men make $125 a month, and there is never any trouble at that mine. Uncle Sam is running the job, and he is a pretty good mine inspector. [Cries of "Tell it, mamma; I can't!"]

There used to be, when I was in Illinois before, a bunch of these black brutes down at Arbuckle, and we had them organized. There was a fellow whose name was "Sy." We have them in the miners' union, as well as in the mines. I asked them whether they were grafting in the union—they got $10 a piece each month, $20 in all. I went down and when they came up reading the financial statement and all those $10 were read, I said, "What is the $10 going for?" They told me. I said, "Get out of camp, I have no use for grafters."

We have them in the union. They have learned the lesson from the mine owners. There was a good old darkey there, and said, "Oh," said Sy, "I done talked to the Lord for a week, and the Lord jest come and whispered in my ear last night, and said, 'Sy, Sy, Sy, I have done had a talk with "Mother" about that graft. Come down to-morrow night,' I said, "O, Lord Jesus, don't fail to let 'Mother' come," and I went. He said, "Jesus didn't lie. Jesus said, 'Mother' come here sure, she take care of that money, and wouldn't let them fellows get it for nothing." At once the fellows said Amen.

So we put a stop to the graft. We have a lot of grafters, too. It is a disease. We have learned the game from the fellows above.

I want you to listen a moment. I want the business men to listen. You business men are up against it. There is a great revolution going on in the industrial world. The Standard Oil Co. owns 86 great department stores in this country. The small business man is beginning to be eliminated. He has got to get down, he can't get up. It is like Carnegie said before the Tariff Commission in Washington. "Gentlemen, I am not bothered about tariff on steel rails." He says, "What concerns me and my class is the right to organize."

The day for the small man is gone, and the day to rise is not here. We want the right to organize. Carnegie said that in a few years—he went into the business with five thousand—he took seven thousand five hundred. He said he knew the time was ripe for steel bridges, and they went into it. He closed out his interest for $300,000,000.

Do you wonder that the steel workers are robbed? When one thief alone can take $300,000,000 and give to a library—to educate our skulls because you didn't get a chance to educate them yourselves.

A fellow said, "I don't think we ought to take those libraries." Yes, take them, and let him build libraries in every town in the country. It is your money. Yet he comes and constructs those libraries as living monuments reddened with the blood of men, women, and children that he robbed.

How did he make $300,000,000? Come with me to Homestead, and I will show you the graves reddened with the blood of men, women, and children. That is where we fixed the Pinkertons, and they have never rose from that day to this. And we will fix the Baldwins in West Virginia.

The Pinkertons were little poodle dogs for the operators. We will fix the Baldwins just the same.

Some fellow said, "You are talking on the porch of the statehouse." That is the very place I want to talk, where what I say will not be perverted.

Senator Dick said, when I met him, "I am delighted to see you, 'Mother' Jones." I said, "I am not delighted to see you." He said, "What is the matter?" I said, "You have passed the Dick military bill to shoot my class down, that is why I wouldn't shake hands with you." That is the way to do business with those fellows. All the papers in the country wrote it up, and he was knocked down off his perch. I will knock a few of these Senators down before I die. [Cries of "Tell it, 'Mother'; I heard it."]

I will tell you. I want you all to be good. [A voice, "Yes; I will." "We are always good."]

They say you are not, but I know you better than the balance do.

Be good; don't drink, only a glass of beer. The parasite bloodsuckers will tell you not to drink beer, because they want to drink it all, you know. They are afraid to tell you to drink for fear there will not be enough for their carcass. [Cries of "The governor takes champagne!"]

He needs it. He gets it from you fellows. He ought to drink it. You pay for it, and as long as he can get it for nothing, any fellow would be a fool not to drink it.

But I want you to be good. We are going to give the governor until to-morrow night. He will not do anything. He could if he would, but the fellows who put him in won't let him. [Cries of "Take him out."]

I don't want him out, because I would have to carry him around. [Applause.]

I want you to keep the peace until I tell you to move, and when I want you every one will come. [Loud applause.]

Now, be good. I don't tell you to go and work for Jesus. Work for yourselves; work for bread. That is the fight we have got. Work for bread. They own our bread.

This fight that you are in is the great industrial revolution that is permeating the heart of men over the world. They see behind the clouds the star that rose in Bethlehem nineteen hundred years ago, that is bringing the message of a better and nobler civilization. We are facing the hour. We are in it, men, the new day; we are here facing that star that will free men and give to the Nation a nobler, grander, higher, truer, purer, better manhood. We are standing on the eve of that mighty hour when the motherhood of the Nation will rise, and instead of clubs or picture shows or excursions, she will devote her life to the training of the human mind, giving to the Nation great men and great women.

I see that hour. I see the star breaking your chains; your chains will be broken, men. You will have to suffer more and more, but it won't be long. There is an awakening among all the nations of the earth.

I want to say, my friends, as Kipling said: He was a military colonel or general in the British Army, and he said:

> We have fed you all thousands of years,
>   And you hail us yet unfed.
> There is not a dollar of your stolen wealth
>   But what marks the graves of workers dead.
> We have given our best to give you rest;
>   You lie on your silken fold.
> O, God, if that be the price of your stolen wealth
>   We have paid it o'er and o'er.
>
> There is never a mine blown skyward now,
>   But our boys are burned to death for gold;
> There is never a wreck on the ocean
>   But what we are its ghastly crew.
> Go count your dead by the forges rail
>   Of the factories where your children lie;

> O, God, if that be the price of your stolen wealth,
>   We pay it a thousand fold.
>
> We have fed you all for thousands of years;
>   That was our doom, you know,
> Since the days they chained us on the field,
>   Till the fight that is now on over the world.
> Aye, you have beaten our lives, our babies and wives,
>   In chains you naked lie.
> O, God, if that be the price we pay for your stolen wealth,
>   We have paid it o'er and o'er.

We are going to stop payment. I want you to quit electing such judges as you have been. This old judge you had here, he used to be your lawyer. When this fight was on he was owned by the corporations. When you wanted him he went off fishing and got a pain in his back. Elect judges and governors from your own ranks.

A doctor said to me in Cincinnati, "Did you ever graduate from a college, Mother Jones?" I said, "I did." He said, "Would you mind telling me?" "No," I said, "I graduated from the college of hard knocks." That is my college; I graduated from that college—hunger, persecution, and suffering—and I wouldn't exchange that college for all the university dudes on the face of God's earth. [Loud applause.]

I know of the wrongs of humanity; I know your aching backs; I know your swimming heads; I know your little children suffer; I know your wives, when I have gone in and found her dead and found the babe nursing at the dead breast, and found the little girl 11 years old taking care of three children. She said, "Mother, will you wake up, baby is hungry and crying?" When I laid my hand on mamma she breathed her last. And the child of 11 had to become a mother to the children.

Oh, men, have you any hearts? Oh, men, do you feel? Oh, men, do you see the judgment day on the throne above, when you will be asked, "Where did you get your gold?" You stole it from these wretches. You murdered, you assassinated, you starved, you burned them to death, that you and your wives might have palaces, and that your wives might go to the seashore. Oh God, men, when I see the horrible picture, when I see the children with their hands off, when I took an army of babies and walked a hundred and thirty miles with a petition to the President of the United States, to pass a bill in Congress to keep these children from being murdered for profit. He had a secret service then all the way to the palace. And now they want to make a President of that man! What is the American Nation coming to?

Manhood, womanhood, can you stand for it? They put reforms in their platforms, but they will get no reform. He promised everything to labor. When we had the strike in Colorado he sent 200 guns to blow our brains out. I don't forget. You do, but I don't. And our women were kicked out like dogs at the point of the bayonet. That is America. They don't do it in Russia. Some women get up with $5 worth of paint on their cheeks and have tooth brushes for their dogs and say, "Oh, them horrible miners," "Oh, that horrible old Mother Jones, that horrible old woman."

I am horrible. I admit, and I want to be to you blood-sucking pirates.

I want you, my boys, to buckle on your armor. This is the fighting age; this is not the age for cowards; put them out of the way.

(At this point "Mother" stopped suddenly and said to some one in the crowd: "Say, are you an operator, with that cigar in your grub?")

Take your medicine, because we are going to get after you, no doubt about it. [Cries from the crowd "Give it to them!"] Yes, I will. [Cries again "Give it to them!"]

I want you to be good. Give the governor time until to-morrow night, and if he don't act then it is up to you. We have all day Saturday, all day Sunday, all day Monday, and Tuesday, and Wednesday if we need it.

We are used to living on little, we can take a crust of bread in our hands and go.

When they started that Civic Federation in New York they got women attached to the Morgan and Rockefeller joint, they wanted to revolutionize the mechanics in Washington. One day I went to their dinner. An Irishman, a machinist, rolled up his sleeves and ran into a restaurant and got a piece of bologna as long as my arm—you know it is black. He got some bread. He put a chunk of the bologna into his mouth and put some bread in his mouth and went out eating. One of these women came along and said, "Oh, my man, don't eat that, it will ruin your stomach; it will give you indigestion." He said, "Oh, hell, the trouble with my stomach is I never get enough to digest."

That is the trouble with half our stomachs. We don't get enough to digest, and when we do get something we are afraid to put it in lest it won't digest.

Go to the "pluck-me" store and get all you can eat. Then you say to "Mirandy"—you say, "O, God, I have a pain in my stomach." You wash yourself, and she holds the water. The mine owner's wife don't hold the water. "Oh, Mirandy, bring the linen to take the corporation hump off my back."

I can't get up to you. I would like to be there, I would give you a hump on your back.

Boys, stay quiet until to-morrow night. I think it would be a good thing to work to-morrow, because the mine owners will need it. The mine commissioner will get a pain in his skull to-night and his wife will give him some "dope." The mine owner's wife is away at the seashore. When she finds no more money coming she will say, "Is there any more money coming?" He will say, "Most of the miners are not working." She will say, "Take the guards and shoot them back into the mines, those horrible fellows."

The governor says, if you don't go to work, said he, in the mines or on the railroads I am going to call the militia, and I will shoot you. So we went. I said we can get ready too. What militia can you get to fight us? Those boys on Paint Creek wouldn't fight us if all the governors in the country wanted you to. I was going yesterday to take dinner with them, but I had something else to do. I am going some day to take dinner with them, and I will convert the whole bunch to my philosophy. I will get them all my way.

Now, be good, boys. Pass the hat around, some of these poor devils want a glass of beer. Get the hat. The mine owner robs them. Get a hat, you fellows of the band.

I want to tell you another thing. These little two by four clerks in the company stores, they sell you five beans for a nickle, sometimes three beans for a nickle. I want to tell you, be civil to those. Don't say anything.

Another thing I want you to do: I want you to go in regular parade, three or four together. The moving-picture man wants to get your picture to send over the country.

(Some one in the crowd asks what the collection is being taken for.)

The hat is for miners who came up here broke, and they want to get a glass of beer. [Loud applause.]

And to pay their way back—and to get a glass of beer. I will give you $5. Get a move on and get something in it.

This day marks the forward march of the workers in the State of West Virginia. Slavery and oppression will gradually die. The National Government will get a record of this meeting. They will say, my friends, this was a peaceful, law-abiding meeting. They will see men of intelligence, that they are not out to destroy but to build. And instead of the horrible homes you have got we will build on their ruins homes for you and your children to live in, and we will build them on the ruins of the dog kennels which they wouldn't keep their mules in. That will bring forth better ideas than the world has had. The day of oppression will be gone. I will be with you whether true or false. I will be with you at midnight or when the battle rages, when the last bullet ceases, but I will be in my joy, as an old saint said:

O, God, of the mighty clan,
　　God grant that the woman who suffered for you,
Suffered not for a coward, but oh, for a man.
　　God grant that the woman who suffered for you,
Suffered not for a coward, but oh, for a fighting man.

[Loud applause.]

Bring the hat in. Is that all you got? [As the hat was handed to her.] "That is all I got."

Go and get some more; that is not enough to go on a strike.

Any of you big fellows got any money in your pockets? If you have shell it out or we will take it out.

(A man coming up out of the crowd: "Here is $10. I will go and borrow more. Shake hands with me, an old union miner. My children are able to take care of themselves, and I will take of myself. Fight, fight, right. I have a good rifle, and I will get more money. If I don't have enough to pay my railroad fare I will walk. I don't care if this was the last cent I had, I will give it to 'Mother' and go and get some more.")

Maybe the governor will give something.

[Cries of "Call him out."]

[Governor, governor, governor.]

The governor is sick. He can't come out. [Applause.]

[Cries of "Better stay sick."]

Hand in the money. [From some one, "The governor is sick."]

MOTHER. Yes; he has got a pain in his stomach.

Go over and form a parade, the moving-picture man wants to take a picture. Go ahead and arrange the parade. Get out and get them in line.

[Cries of "Gov. Glasscock."]

Hush up, the poor fellow is sick.

[Cries for "Houston, Houston."]

[Cries of "Gone to the hospital."]

Now, let us go home. Be good boys. I am coming down to the camps and see you.

Emma Goldman

(1869–1940)

ADDRESS TO THE JURY
July 9, 1917

Emma Goldman was widely considered one of the most dangerously eloquent and inflammatory public speakers of her time. An ardent feminist and anarchist, Goldman spoke out for free speech, birth control, and social justice, often finding herself at odds with authority wherever she spoke. In 1917 Goldman, along with Alexander Berkman, was arrested and charged with conspiracy to obstruct the draft for her work as a founder of the No-Conscription League, an organization designed to convince young men not to fight in World War I. The following speech is Goldman's defense from that trial, during which she acted as her own counsel. After deliberating only thirty-nine minutes, the jury found Goldman and Berkman guilty, and they were both given two-year jail sentences in addition to $10,000 fines.

GENTLEMEN OF THE JURY: On the day after our arrest it was given out by the Marshal's office and the District Attorney's office that the two "big fish" of the no-conscription activities were now in the hands of the authorities, that there would be no more troublemakers and dangerous disturbers, that the government will be able to go on in the highly democratic method of conscripting American manhood for European slaughter. It is a great pity, it seems to me, that the Marshal and the District Attorney have used such a flimsy net to make their catch. The moment they attempted to land the fish on shore the net broke. Indeed the net proved that it was not able and strong enough to hold the fish. The sensational arrest of the defendants and the raid of the defendants' offices would have satisfied the famous circus men, Barnum & Bailey. Imagine, if you can, a dozen stalwart warriors rushing up two flights of stairs to find the two defendants,

99

Alexander Berkman and Emma Goldman, in their separate offices quietly seated at their desks, wielding not the gun or the bomb or the club or the sword, but only such a simple and insignificant thing as a pen. As a matter of fact two officers equipped with a warrant would have sufficed to arrest us two, for I take it that we are well known to the police department and the police department will bear me out that at no time have we run away or attempted to run away, that at no time have we offered any resistance to an arrest, that at no time did we keep in hiding under the bed. We have always frankly and squarely faced the issue. But it was necessary to stage a sensational arrest so that Marshal McCarthy and the attorney should go down to posterity and receive immortality. It was necessary to raid offices of the *Blast* and the No-Conscription League and *Mother Earth,* although without a search warrant, which was never shown to us. I ask you, gentlemen of the jury, should it be customary from the point of view of law to discriminate in the case of people merely because they have opinions which do not appeal to you? What is a scrap of paper in the form of a search warrant, when it is a question of raiding the offices of Anarchists or arresting Anarchists? Would the gentlemen who came with Marshall McCarthy have dared to go into the offices of Morgan or of Rockefeller or any of these men without a search warrant? They never showed us the search warrant, although we asked them for it. Nevertheless, they turned our office into a battlefield, so that when they were through with it it looked like invaded Belgium, with only the distinction that the invaders were not Prussian barbarians but good patriots who were trying to make New York safe for democracy.

The first act of this marvelous comedy having been properly staged by carrying off the villains in a madly rushing automobile which came near crushing life in its way, merely because Marshal McCarthy said "I am the Marshal of the United States," he even reprimanding officers on the automobile should not have rushed at such violent speed—I say the first act having been finished by locking the villains up, the second act appeared on the scene. And the second act, gentlemen of the jury, consisted not in prosecution but in persecution. Here are two people arrested, known to the police department, having lived in New York City for nearly thirty years, never having offered resistance to an arrest, always facing the issue. And yet we were placed under $50,000 bail, although the principal witness in the Cruger case is held only in $7,000 bail. Wy were we placed under $50,000 bail? Because the District Attorney knew that it would be difficult to raise that bail and therefore out of personal spite made us stay in the Tombs instead of enjoying our liberty. And furthermore, not only did the District Attorney and the prosecution insist upon $50,000 bail, but when we produced a man whose property is rated at $300,000 in this city his real estate was refused. Why? Because the District Attorney suddenly remembered that he needed 48 hours to look into the man's reputation—knowing perfectly well that we were to go on trial on Wednesday, and yet not permitting the defendant, Alexander Berkman, to get out, although we had relied on an authentic and absolutely secure bail. So that I say that the second act, gentlemen of the jury, demonstrated that it was not only to be a case of prosecution, that it was also to be a case of persecution.

And finally the third act which was played in this court and which you, gentlemen of the jury, witnessed last week. I may say here that it is to be regretted indeed that the District Attorney knows nothing of dramatic construction, otherwise he would have supplied himself with better dramatic material, he would have used better acts in the play to sustain the continuity of the comedy. But the District Attorney is not supposed to know anything about modern drama or the construction of modern drama.

Now then you have already been told and I am sure you will be charged by His Honor that the indictment against us is, having conspired and having used overt acts to carry out the conspiracy to induce men of conscriptable age not to register. That is the indictment and you cannot and you may not render a verdict for anything else, no matter what material came up in this court during the last week or ten days. As to the conspiracy: imagine, if you please, people engaged along similar lines for nearly thirty years, always standing out against war, whether that war was in China or Japan or Russia or England or Germany or America, always insisting with the great essayist Carlyle, that all wars are wars among thieves who are too cowardly to fight and who therefore induce the young manhood of the whole world to do the fighting for them—that is our standing; we have proved it by evidence, we have proved it by witnesses, we have proved it by our own position, that always and forever we have stood up against war, because we say that the war going on in the world is for the further enslavement of the people, for the further placing of them under the yoke of a military tyranny; imagine also people who for thirty years in succession have stood out against militarism, who claim militarism is costly and useless and brutalizing to every country; imagine us standing for years, and especially since conscription was declared in England and the fight began in Australia and conscription was there defeated by the brave and determined and courageous position of the Australian people; imagine that since that time we have been against conscription, then say how there can possibly be a conspiracy when people merely continue in their work which they have carried on for thirty years and for which they have spoken in different meetings and by letters! What kind of conspiracy is that? Was there any need of a conspiracy if we really had wanted to tell young men not to register? I insist that the prosecution has failed utterly, has failed miserably to prove the charge on the indictment of a conspiracy.

As to the meeting of May 18th: it was dragged in here only for reasons known to the prosecution, otherwise I can't understand why that meeting played such an important part. No matter what we would have said at that meeting, no matter what language we would have used, that meeting cannot constitute an overt act, because although it is true that the draft law was passed on the 18th, it is equally true that it was not made a law until the President of the United States signed that law. And the President of the United States did not sign it until late that evening, at the time when we had the meeting and couldn't have any idea or knowledge as to whether he was going to sign it. So the meeting of the 18th is utterly irrelevant. But since the meeting came in it is necessary to emphasize one or two points. And I mean to do so, because it concerns the defendant Emma Goldman. The main thing upon which evidently the prosecution concentrated is that the reporter credited the defendant Emma Goldman with saying, "We believe in violence and we will use violence." Gentlemen of the jury, if there were no other proof to absolutely discredit this particular line and sentence and expression, there would yet be the following reasons: In the first place, I have been on the public platform for 27 years and one of the things that I am particularly careful of in my speeches is that they shall be coherent and shall be logical. The speeches delivered on that evening, on May 18th, absolutely excluded the necessity of using the expression, "We believe in violence and we will use violence." I couldn't have used it, as an experienced speaker, because it would merely have made the whole speech nonsensical, it would have dragged in something which was irrelevant to the body of the speech or the material used. That is one of the reasons why I never at that meeting said, "We believe in violence and we will use violence."

I am a social student. It is my business in life to ascertain the cause of our social evils and of our social difficulties. As a student of social wrongs it is my business to diagnose a wrong. To simply condemn the man who has committed an act of political violence, in order to save my own skin, would be just as pardonable as it would be on the part of the physician who is called to diagnose a case, to condemn the patient because the patient had tuberculosis or cancer or any other disease. The honest, earnest, sincere physician diagnoses a case, he does not only prescribe medicine, he tries to find out the cause of the disease. And if the patient is at all capable as to means, he will tell the patient, "Get out of this putrid air, get out of the factory, get out of the place where your lungs are being infected." He will not merely give him medicines. He will tell him the cause of the disease. And that is precisely my position in regard to violence. That is what I have said on all platforms. I have attempted to explain the cause and the reason for acts of political violence.

And what is the cause? Is it conditioned in the individual who commits an act of individual violence? It is not. An act of political violence at the bottom is the culminating result of organized violence on top. It is the result of violence which expresses itself in war, which expresses itself in capital punishment, which expresses itself in courts, which expresses itself in prisons, which expresses itself in kicking and hounding people for the only crime they are guilty of: of having been born poor. So that after all when we come to consider an act of political violence committed by an individual, I take it, gentlemen of the jury, that you are conversant with history and that you know that not only a stray Anarchist here and there, but rebels of every movement in Ireland, in France, in Russia, in Italy, in Spain, all over the world, even in passive India, the country which has the most wonderful civilization and rests upon passive resistance—even in that country, men were driven to acts of violence by organized violence on top. So, as I said in one of the evidences we have given, we say with the greatest psychologist living, Havelock Ellis, that an act of political violence committed by an individual is the result of social wrong and social injustice and political oppression. Wherever there is political liberty—and I can demonstrate it in the Scandinavian countries: has there been any act of violence committed in Norway, in Sweden, in Denmark, in Holland—why are there no acts of violence there? Because the government doesn't only preach free speech and free press and assembly, but lives up to it. There was no need to be driven into acts of violence. So, gentlemen, I say with Havelock Ellis that the political offender or the "political criminal," as you choose to call him, is so not because of criminal tendency, not because of personal gain, not because of personal aggrandizement, but because he loves humanity too well; because he cannot face wrong and injustice and because he cannot enjoy his meal when he knows that America is getting rich on two million wage-slave children who are ground into dust and into money and power.

And so, gentlemen, I have explained the act. I have explained the act. Does that mean advocating the act? If that is your version—and I can't believe that it will be—I say, gentlemen of the jury, that you might as well condemn Jesus for having defended the prostitute Mary

Magdalen, you might as well say that he advocated prostitution because he said to the mob on that occasion: "Let him among you that is without sin, cast the first stone." I refuse to cast the stone at the "political criminal," if he may be called so. I take his place with him because he has been driven to revolt, because his life-breath has been choked up. And if I am to pay with prison for that, if I am to pay with my life-breath for that, gentlemen of the jury, I shall be ready at any time to take the consequences. But I refuse to be tried on trumped-up charges and I refuse to be convicted by perjured testimony for something which I haven't said, when it had absolutely no relation whatever to the indictment as stated, that we conspired and agreed to conspire and used overt acts to tell people not to register.

Gentlemen of the jury, the meeting of May 18 was called for an express purpose and for that purpose only. It was called to voice the position of the conscientious objector who, as far as America is concerned, was a new type of humanity. Oh I know that we should be expected to call the conscientious objector, just as he is being called by the papers, a "slacker," a "coward," a "shirker." These are cheap names, gentlemen of the jury. To call a man a name proves nothing whatever. What is the conscientious objector? I am a conscientious objector. What is he? He is impelled by what President Wilson said in his speech on the 3rd of February, 1917; he is impelled by the force of righteous passion for justice, which is the bulwark and mainstay and basis of all our existence and of all our liberty. That is the force which impels the conscientious objector: a righteous passion for justice. The conscientious objector, rightly or wrongly—that is a thing which you will have to argue with him—does not believe in war, not because he is a coward or a shirker, not because he doesn't want to stand responsible, but because he insists that, belonging to the people whence he has come and to whom he owes life, it is his place to stand on the side of the people, for the people, and by the people and not on the side of the governing classes. And that is what we did at that particular meeting. We voiced the position of the conscientious objector. But I reiterate once more, so you may not overlook it: that whatever we said on the 18th of May has no bearing whatever on the indictment for conspiracy, because that meeting took place before the president signed that bill.

Gentlemen of the jury, when we examined talesmen we asked whether you would be prejudiced against us when it was proved that we were engaged in an agitation for unpopular ideas. You were instructed by the court to say "if they were within the law." But there was one thing I am sorry that the Court did not tell you. It is this: that there has never been any ideal—though ever so humane and peace-

ful—introduced for human betterment which in its place and in its
time was considered within the law. I know that many of you believe
in the teachings of Jesus. I want to call your attention to the fact that
Jesus was put to death because he was not within the law. I know that
all of you are Americans and patriots. Please bear in mind that those
who fought and bled for whatever liberty you have, those who established the Declaration of Independence, those who established the
constitutional right of free speech—that they were not within the
law; that they were the Anarchists of their time; that they wrote a
famous document known as the Declaration of Independence, a
document indeed so great that it is evidently considered dangerous to
this day, because a boy was given ninety days in a New York court
for distributing a leaflet of quotations from the Declaration of
Independence. They were not within the law. Those men were the
rebels and the Anarchists. And what is more important, they not only
believed in violence but they used violence when they threw the tea
into Boston harbor.

Furthermore, your country and in a measure my country—my
country out of choice—is now allied with France. Need I call your
attention to the fact that the French republic is due to the men who
were not within the law? Why, friends, even the man who is responsible for the stirring music of the Marseillaise, which unfortunately has
been deteriorating into a war tune—even Camille Desmoulins was
not within the law, was considered a criminal. And finally, gentlemen, on the very day when we are tried for a conspiracy, when we
are tried for overt acts, our city and its representatives were receiving
with festivities and with music the Russian Commission. Every one
of the Russian commissioners is what you would choose to call an
ex-political criminal. Every one of them had been in exile or in
prison. As a matter of fact, gentlemen, the tree of Russian liberty is
watered with the blood of Russian martyrs.

So no great idea in its beginning can ever be within the law. How
can it be within the law? The law is stationary. The law is fixed. The
law is a chariot wheel which binds us all regardless of conditions or
circumstances or place or time. The law does not even make an attempt to go into the complexity of the human soul which drives a
man to despair or to insanity, out of hunger or out of indignation,
into a political act. But progress is ever changing, progress is ever
renewing, progress has nothing to do with fixity. And in its place and
in its time every great ideal for human reconstruction, for a reconstruction of society and the regeneration of the race—every great idea
was considered extralegal, illegal, in its time and place. And so I must
refer to Havelock Ellis when he said that the political criminal is the

hero and the martyr and the saint of the new era. Hence the country that locks up men and women who will stand up for an ideal—what chance is there for that country and for the future and for the young generation, a country that has not in her midst dangerous disturbers and troublemakers who can see further than their time and propagate a new idea?

Well, gentlemen, I take it that perhaps the prosecution will say that that means propagating dangerous and seditious ideas in this time of war and patriotism. Maybe it does, gentlemen of the jury. But that doesn't prove that we are responsible for the existence of such ideas. You might as well condemn the very stars that are hanging in the heavens eternally and inalienably and unchangeably for all time, as to accuse us or find us guilty because we propagate certain ideas. Gentlemen of the jury, I wish to say right here we respect your patriotism. We wouldn't, even if we could, want you to change one single iota of what patriotism means to you. But may there not be two kinds of patriotism, just as there are two interpretations of liberty, the kind of liberty which is real liberty in action, and the kind which has been placed on a document and is dug out once a year on the 4th of July and is not allowed to exist for the rest of the year? And so, gentlemen, I wish to emphasize this very important fact, because I know how you feel on the war, I know what patriotism means to you: that the mere accident of birth or the mere fact that you have taken out citizens' papers does not make a man necessarily a patriot. Who is the real patriot, or rather what is the kind of patriotism that we represent? The kind of patriotism we represent is the kind of patriotism which loves America with open eyes. Our relation toward America is the same as the relation of a man who loves a woman, who is enchanted by her beauty and yet who cannot be blind to her defects. And so I wish to state here, in my own behalf and in behalf of hundreds of thousands whom you decry and state to be antipatriotic, that we love America, we love her beauty, we love her riches, we love her mountains and her forests, and above all we love the people who have produced her wealth and riches, who have created all her beauty, we love the dreamers and the philosophers and the thinkers who are giving America liberty. But that must not make us blind to the social faults of America. That cannot make us deaf to the discords in America. That cannot compel us to be inarticulate to the terrible wrongs committed in the name of the country.

We simply insist, regardless of all protests to the contrary, that this war is not a war for democracy. If it were a war for the purpose of making democracy safe for the world, we would say that democracy must first be safe for America before it can be safe for the world. So in a measure I say, gentlemen, that we are greater patriots than those who shoot off firecrackers and say that democracy should be given to the world. By all means let us give democracy to the world. But for the present we are very poor in democracy. Free speech is suppressed. Free assemblies are broken up by uniformed gangsters, one after another. Women and girls at meetings are insulted by soldiers under this "democracy." And therefore we say that we are woefully poor in democracy at home. How can we be generous in giving democracy to the world? So we say, gentlemen of the jury, our crime if crime there be, is not having in any way conspired to tell young men not to register, or having committed overt acts. Our crime, if crime there be, consists in pointing out the real cause of the present war.

I wish to state to you here that whatever your verdict is going to be it cannot have a possible effect upon the tremendous storm brewing in the United States. And the storm has not been created by two people, Alexander Berkman and Emma Goldman. You credit us with too much power altogether. That storm was created by the conditions themselves, by the fact that the people before election were promised that they would be kept out of war and after election they were dragged into war. Gentlemen of the jury, your verdict cannot affect the growing discontent of the American people. Neither can it affect the conscientious objector to whom human life is sacred and who would rather be shot than take the life of another human being. Of course your verdict is going to affect us. It will affect us only temporarily. And it will affect us physically: it cannot affect our spirit, gentlemen of the jury, whether we are found guilty or whether we are placed in jail. Nothing will be changed in our spirit. Nothing will be changed in our ideas. For even if we were convicted and found guilty and the penalty were, to be placed against a wall and shot dead, I should nevertheless cry out with the great Luther: "Here I am and here I stand and I cannot do otherwise."

And so, gentlemen, in conclusion let me tell you that my co-defendant, Mr. Berkman, was right when he said the eyes of America are upon you. And they are upon you not because of sympathy for us or agreement with Anarchism. They are upon you because it must be decided sooner or later. Are we justified in telling people that we will give them democracy in Europe, when we have no democracy here? Shall free speech and free assemblage, shall criticism and opinion, which even the espionage bill did not include—shall that be destroyed? Shall it be a shadow of the past, the great historic American past? Shall it be trampled underfoot by any detective, any policeman, anyone, who decides upon it? Or shall free speech and free press and free assemblage continue to be the heritage of the American people?

And so, gentlemen of the jury, whatever your verdict will be, as far as we are concerned, nothing will be changed. I have held ideas all my life. I have publicly held my ideas for 27 years. Nothing on earth would ever make me change my ideas except one thing; and that is, if you will prove to me that our position is wrong, untenable, or lacking in historic fact. But never would I change my ideas because I am found guilty. I must say in the great words of two great Americans, undoubtedly not unknown to you gentlemen of the jury, and that is Ralph Waldo Emerson and Henry David Thoreau: when Henry David Thoreau was placed in prison for refusing to pay taxes he was visited by Ralph Waldo Emerson and Emerson said: "David, what are you doing in jail?" and Thoreau said: "Ralph, what are you doing outside, when people are in jail for their ideals?" And so, gentlemen of the jury, I do not wish to influence you. I do not wish to appeal to your passions. I do not wish to influence you by the fact that I am a woman. I have no such desires and no such designs. I take it that you are sincere enough and honest enough and brave enough to render a verdict according to your convictions, beyond the shadow of a reasonable doubt.

Please forget that we are Anarchists. Forget that we said that we propagated violence. Forget that something appeared in *Mother Earth* when I was thousands of miles away three years ago. Forget all that. And merely consider the evidence. Have we been engaged in a conspiracy? Has that conspiracy been proved; have we committed overt acts; have those overt acts been proved? We for the defense say they have not been proved. And therefore your verdict must be not guilty.

Margaret Sanger

(1879–1966)

A MORAL NECESSITY FOR BIRTH CONTROL
November 18, 1921

Margaret Sanger is best remembered as the founder of the American Birth Control League, the pro-birth control organization that would go on to become Planned Parenthood. Educated and employed as a nurse, Sanger left the profession to become a birth control advocate, setting up the first birth control clinic in the United States in 1917. The following speech was delivered on numerous occasions for the American Birth Control League throughout 1921 and 1922.

> I went to the Garden of Love,
>   And saw what I never had seen;
> A Chapel was built in the midst,
>   Where I used to play on the green.
>
> And the gates of this Chapel were shut,
>   And "Thou shalt not" writ over the door;
> So I turned to the Garden of Love
>   That so many sweet flowers bore.
>
> And I saw it was filled with graves,
>   And tombstones where flowers should be;
> And priests in black gowns were walking their rounds,
>   And binding with briars my joys and desires.
>   WILLIAM BLAKE

ORTHODOX OPPOSITION to Birth Control is formulated in the official protest of the National Council of Catholic Women against the resolution passed by the New York State Federation of Women's Clubs which favored the removal of all obstacles to the spread of information regarding practical methods of Birth Control. The Catholic state-

109

ment completely embodies traditional opposition to Birth Control. It affords a striking contrast by which we may clarify and justify the ethical necessity for this new instrument of civilization as the most effective basis for practical and scientific morality. "The authorities at Rome have again and again declared that all positive methods of this nature are immoral and forbidden," states the National Council of Catholic Women. "There is no question of the lawfulness of birth restriction through abstinence from the relations which result in conception. The immorality of Birth Control as it is practised and commonly understood, consists in the evils of the particular method employed. These are all contrary to the moral law because they are unnatural, being a perversion of a natural function. Human faculties are used in such a way as to frustrate the natural end for which these faculties were created. This is always intrinsically wrong—as wrong as lying and blasphemy. No supposed beneficial consequence can make good a practice which is, in itself, immoral. . . .

"The evil results of the practice of Birth Control are numerous. Attention will be called here to only three. The first is the degradation of the marital relation itself, since the husband and wife who indulge in any form of this practice come to have a lower idea of married life. They cannot help coming to regard each other to a great extent as mutual instruments of sensual gratification, rather than as cooperators with the Creator in bringing children into the world. This consideration may be subtle but it undoubtedly represents the facts.

"In the second place, the deliberate restriction of the family through these immoral practices deliberately weakens self-control and the capacity for self-denial, and increases the love of ease and luxury. The best indication of this is that the small family is much more prevalent in the classes that are comfortable and well-to-do than among those whose material advantages are moderate or small. The theory of the advocates of Birth Control is that those parents who are comfortably situated should have a large number of children (*sic!*) while the poor should restrict their off-spring to a much smaller number. This theory does not work, for the reason that each married couple have their own idea of what constitutes unreasonable hardship in the matter of bearing and rearing children. A large proportion of the parents who are addicted to Birth Control practices are sufficiently provided with worldly goods to be free from apprehension on the economic side; nevertheless, they have small families because they are disinclined to undertake the other burdens involved in bringing up a more numerous family. A practice which tends to produce such exaggerated notions of what constitutes hardship, which leads men and women to cherish such a degree of ease, makes inevitably for inefficiency, a decline in the capacity to endure and to achieve, and for a general social decadence.

"Finally, Birth Control leads sooner or later to a decline in population. . . ." (The case of France is instanced.) But it is essentially the moral question that alarms the Catholic women, for the statement concludes: "The further effect of such proposed legislation will inevitably be a lowering both of public and private morals. What the fathers of this country termed indecent and forbade the mails to carry, will, if such legislation is carried through, be legally decent. The purveyors of sexual license and immorality will have the opportunity to send almost anything they care to write through the mails on the plea that it is sex information. Not only the married but also the unmarried will be thus affected; the ideals of the young contaminated and lowered. The morals of the entire nation will suffer.

"The proper attitude of Catholics . . . is clear. They should watch and oppose all attempts in state legislatures and in Congress to repeal the laws which now prohibit the dissemination of information concerning Birth Control. Such information will be spread only too rapidly despite existing laws. To repeal these would greatly accelerate this deplorable movement."

The Catholic position has been stated in an even more extreme form by Archbishop Patrick J. Hayes of the archdiocese of New York. In a "Christmas Pastoral" this dignitary even went to the extent of declaring that "even though some little angels in the flesh, through the physical or mental deformities of their parents, may appear to human eyes hideous, misshapen, a blot on civilized society, we must not lose sight of this Christian thought that under and within such visible malformation, lives an immortal soul to be saved and glorified for all eternity among the blessed in heaven."

With the type of moral philosophy expressed in this utterance, we need not argue. It is based upon traditional ideas that have had the practical effect of making this world a vale of tears. Fortunately such words carry no weight with those who can bring free and keen as well as noble minds to the consideration of the matter. To them the idealism of such an utterance appears crude and cruel. The menace to civilization of such orthodoxy, if it be orthodoxy, lies in the fact that its powerful exponents may be for a time successful not merely in influencing the conduct of their adherents but in checking freedom of thought and discussion. To this, with all the vehemence of emphasis at our command, we object. From what Archibishop Hayes believes concerning the future blessedness in Heaven of the souls of those who are born into this world as hideous and misshapen beings he has a right to seek such consolation as may be obtained; but we who are trying to better the conditions of this world believe that a healthy, happy human race is more in keeping with the laws of God, than disease, misery and poverty perpetuating itself generation after generation. Furthermore, while conceding to Catholic or other churchmen full freedom to preach their own doctrines, whether of theology or morals, nevertheless when they attempt to carry these ideas into legislative acts and force their opinions and codes upon the non-Catholics, we consider such action an interference with the principles of democracy and we have a right to protest.

Religious propaganda against Birth Control is crammed with contradiction and fallacy. It refutes itself. Yet it brings the opposing views into vivid contrast. In stating these differences we should make clear that advocates of Birth Control are not seeking to attack the Catholic church. We quarrel with that church, however, when it seeks to assume authority over non-Catholics and to dub their behavior immoral because they do not conform to the dictatorship of Rome. The question of bearing and rearing children we hold is the concern of the mother and the potential mother. If she delegates the responsibility, the ethical education, to an external authority, that is her affair. We object, however, to the State or the Church which appoints itself as arbiter and dictator in this sphere and attempts to force unwilling women into compulsory maternity.

When Catholics declare that "the authorities at Rome have again and again declared that all positive methods of this nature are immoral and forbidden," they do so upon the assumption that morality consists in conforming to laws laid down and enforced by external authority, in submission to decrees and dicta imposed from without. In this case, they decide in a wholesale manner the conduct of millions, demanding of them not the intelligent exercise of their own individual judgment and discrimination, but unquestioning submission and conformity to dogma. The Church thus takes the place of all-powerful parents, and demands of its children merely that they should obey. In my belief such a philosophy hampers the development of individual intelligence. Morality then becomes a more or less successful attempt to conform to a code, instead of an attempt to bring reason and intelligence to bear upon the solution of each individual human problem.

But, we read on, Birth Control methods are not merely contrary to "moral law," but forbidden because they are "unnatural," being "the perversion of a natural function." This, of course, is the weakest link in the whole chain. Yet "there is no question of the lawfulness of birth restriction through abstinence"—as though abstinence itself were not unnatural! For more than a thousand years the Church was occupied with the problem of imposing abstinence on its priesthood, its most educated and trained body of men, educated to look upon asceticism as the finest ideal; it took one thousand years to convince the Catholic priesthood that abstinence was "natural" or practicable. Nevertheless, there is still this talk of abstinence, self-control, and self-denial, almost in the same breath with the condemnation of Birth Control as "unnatural."

If it is our duty to act as "cooperators with the Creator" to bring children into the world, it is difficult to say at what point our behavior is "unnatural." If it is immoral and "unnatural" to prevent an unwanted life from coming into existence, is it not immoral and "unnatural" to remain unmarried from the age of puberty? Such casuistry is unconvincing and feeble. We need only point out that rational intelligence is also a "natural" function, and that it is as imperative for us to use the faculties of judgment, criticism, discrimination of choice, selection and control, all the faculties of the intelligence, as it is to use those of reproduction. It is certainly dangerous "to frustrate the natural ends for which these faculties were created." This, also, is always intrinsically wrong—as wrong as lying and blasphemy—and infinitely more devastating. Intelligence is as natural to us as any other faculty, and it is fatal to moral development and growth to refuse to use it and to delegate to others the solution of our individual problems. The evil will not be that one's conduct is divergent from current and conventional moral codes. There may be every outward evidence of conformity, but this agreement may be arrived at, by the restriction and suppression of subjective desires, and the more or less successful attempt at mere conformity. Such "morality" would conceal an inner conflict. The fruits of this conflict would be neurosis and hysteria on the one hand; or concealed gratification of suppressed desires on the other, with a resultant hypocrisy and cant. True morality cannot be based on conformity. There must be no conflict between subjective desire and outward behavior.

To object to these traditional and churchly ideas does not by any means imply that the doctrine of Birth Control is anti-Christian. On the contrary, it may be profoundly in accordance with the Sermon on the Mount. One of the greatest living theologians and most penetrating students of the problems of civilization is of this opinion. In an address delivered before the Eugenics Education Society of London, William Ralph Inge, the Very Reverend Dean of St. Paul's Cathedral, London, pointed out that the doctrine of Birth Control was to be interpreted as of the very essence of Christianity.

"We should be ready to give up all our theories," he asserted, "if science proved that we were on the wrong lines. And we can understand, though we profoundly disagree with, those who oppose us on the grounds of authority. . . . We know where we are with a man who says, 'Birth Control is forbidden by God; we prefer poverty, unemployment, war, the physical, intellectual and moral degeneration of the people, and a high death rate to any interference with the universal command to be fruitful and multiply'; but we have no patience with those who say that we can have unrestricted and unregulated propagation without those consequences. It is a great part of our work to press home to the public mind the alternative that lies before us. Either rational selection must take the place of the natural selection which the modern State will not allow to act, or we must go on deteriorating. When we can convince the public of this, the opposition of organized religion will soon collapse or become ineffective."

Dean Inge effectively answers those who have objected to the methods of Birth Control is "immoral" and in contradiction and inimical to the teachings of Christ. Incidentally he claims that those who are not blinded by prejudices recognize that "Christianity aims at saving the soul—the personality, the nature, of man, not his body or his environment. According to Christianity, a man is saved, not by what he has, or knows, or does, but by what he is. It treats all the apparatus of life with a disdain as great as that of the biologist; so long as a man is inwardly healthy, it cares very little whether he is rich or poor, learned or simple, and even whether he is happy, or unhappy. It attaches no importance to quantitative measurements of any kind. The Christian does not gloat over favorable trade-statistics, nor congratulate himself on the disparity between the number of births and deaths. For him . . . the test of the welfare of a country is the quality of the human beings whom it produces. Quality is everything, quantity is nothing. And besides this, the Christian conception of a kingdom of God upon earth teaches us to turn our eyes to the future, and to think of the welfare of posterity as a thing which concerns us as much as that of our own generation. This welfare, as conceived by Christianity, is of course something different from external prosperity; it is to be the victory of intrinsic worth and healthiness over all the false ideals and deep-seated diseases which at present spoil civilization."

"It is not political religion with which I am concerned," Dean Inge explained, "but the convictions of really religious persons; and I do not think that we need despair of converting them to our views."

Dean Inge believes Birth Control is an essential part of Eugenics, and an essential part of Christian morality. On this point he asserts: "We do wish to remind our orthodox and conservative friends that the Sermon on the Mount contains some admirably clear and unmistakable eugenic precepts. 'Do men gather grapes of thorns, or figs of thistles? A corrupt tree cannot bring forth good fruit, neither can a good tree bring forth evil fruit. Every tree which bringeth not forth good fruit is hewn down, and cast into the fire.' We wish to apply these words not only to the actions of individuals, which spring from their characters, but to the character of individuals, which spring from their inherited qualities. This extension of the scope of the maxim seems to me quite legitimate. Men do not gather grapes of thorns. As our proverb says, you cannot make a silk purse out of a sow's ear. If we believe this, and do not act upon it by trying to move public opinion towards giving social reform, education and religion a better material to work upon, we are sinning against the light, and not doing our best to bring in the Kingdom of God upon earth."

As long as sexual activity is regarded in a dualistic and contradictory light,—in which it is revealed either as the instrument by which men and women "cooperate with the Creator" to bring children into the world, on the one hand; and on the other, as the sinful instrument of self-gratification, lust and sensuality, there is bound to be an endless conflict in human conduct, producing ever increasing misery, pain and injustice. In crystallizing and codifying this contradiction, the Church not only solidified its own power over men but reduced women to the most abject and prostrate slavery. It was essentially a morality that would not "work." The sex instinct in the human race is too strong to be bound by the dictates of any church. The church's failure, its century after century of failure, is now evident on every side: for, having convinced men and women that only in its badly propagative phase is sexual expression legitimate, the teachings of the Church have driven sex under ground, into secret channels, strengthened the conspiracy of silence, concentrated men's thoughts upon the "lusts of the body," have sown, cultivated and reaped a crop of bodily and mental diseases, and developed a society congenitally and almost hopelessly unbalanced. How is any progress to be made, how is any human expression or education possible when women and men are taught to combat and resist their natural impulses and to despise their bodily functions?

Humanity, we are glad to realize, is rapidly freeing itself from this "morality" imposed upon it by its self-appointed and self-perpetuating masters. From a hundred different points the imposing edifice of this "morality" has been and is being attacked. Sincere and thoughtful defenders and exponents of the teachings of Christ now acknowledge the falsity of the traditional codes and their malignant influence upon the moral and physical well-being of humanity.

Ecclesiastical opposition to Birth Control on the part of certain representatives of the Protestant churches, based usually on quotations from the Bible, is equally invalid, and for the same reason. The attitude of the more intelligent and enlightened clergy has been well and

succinctly expressed by Dean Inge, who, referring to the ethics of
Birth Control, writes: "*This is emphatically a matter in which every man
and woman must judge for themselves, and must refrain from judging others.*"
We must not neglect the important fact that it is not merely in the
practical results of such a decision, not in the small number of children, not even in the healthier and better cared for children, not in
the possibility of elevating the living conditions of the individual family, that the ethical value of Birth Control alone lies. Precisely because
the practice of Birth Control does demand the exercise of decision,
the making of choice, the use of the reasoning powers, is it an instrument of moral education as well as of hygienic and racial advance. It
awakens the attention of parents to their potential children. It forces
upon the individual consciousness the question of the standards of
living. In a profound manner it protects and reasserts the inalienable
rights of the child-to-be.

Psychology and the outlook of modern life are stressing the growth
of independent responsibility and discrimination as the true basis of
ethics. The old traditional morality, with its train of vice, disease,
promiscuity and prostitution, is in reality dying out, killing itself off
because it is too irresponsible and too dangerous to individual and
social well-being. The transition from the old to the new, like all
fundamental changes, is fraught with many dangers. But it is a revolution that cannot be stopped.

The smaller family, with its lower infant mortality rate, is, in more
definite and concrete manner than many actions outwardly deemed
"moral," the expression of moral judgment and responsibility. It is the
assertion of a standard of living, inspired by the wish to obtain a fuller
and more expressive life for the children than the parents have enjoyed. If the morality or immorality of any course of conduct is to be
determined by the motives which inspire it, there is evidently at the
present day no higher morality than the intelligent practice of Birth
Control.

The immorality of many who practise Birth Control lies in not daring to preach what they practise. What is the secret of the hypocrisy
of the well-to-do, who are willing to contribute generously to charities and philanthropies, who spend thousands annually in the upkeep
and sustenance of the delinquent, the defective and the dependent;
and yet join the conspiracy of silence that prevents the poorer classes
from learning how to improve their conditions, and elevate their
standards of living? It is as though they were to cry: "We'll give you
anything except the thing you ask for—the means whereby you may
become responsible and self-reliant in your own lives."

The brunt of this injustice falls on women, because the old traditional morality is the invention of men. "No religion, no physical or moral code," wrote the clear-sighted George Drysdale, "proposed by one sex for the other, can be really suitable. Each must work out its laws for itself in every department of life." In the moral code developed by the Church, women have been so degraded that they have been habituated to look upon themselves through the eyes of men. Very imperfectly have women developed their own self-consciousness, the realization of their tremendous and supreme position in civilization. Women can develop this power only in one way; by the exercise of responsibility, by the exercise of judgment, reason or discrimination. They need ask for no "rights." They need only assert power. Only by the exercise of self-guidance and intelligent self-direction can that inalienable, supreme, pivotal power be expressed. More than ever in history women need to realize that nothing can ever come to us from another. Everything we attain we must owe to ourselves. Our own spirit must vitalize it. Our own heart must feel it. For we are not passive machines. We are not to be lectured, guided and molded this way or that. We are alive and intelligent, we women, no less than men, and we must awaken to the essential realization that we are living beings, endowed with will, choice, comprehension, and that every step in life must be taken at our own initiative.

Moral and sexual balance in civilization will only be established by the assertion and expression of power on the part of women. This power will not be found in any futile seeking for economic independence or in the aping of men in industrial and business pursuits, nor by joining battle for the so called "single standard." Woman's power can only be expressed and make itself felt when she refuses the task of bringing unwanted children into the world to be exploited in industry and slaughtered in wars. When we refuse to produce battalions of babies to be exploited; when we declare to the nation; "Show us that the best possible chance in life is given to every child now brought into the world, before you cry for more! At present our children are a glut on the market. You hold infant life cheap. Help us to make the world a fit place for children. When you have done this, we will bear you children,—then we shall be true women." The new morality will express this power and responsibility on the part of women.

"With the realization of the moral responsibility of women," writes Havelock Ellis, "the natural relations of life spring back to their due biological adjustment. Motherhood is restored to its natural sacredness. It becomes the concern of the woman herself, and not of society nor any individual, to determine the conditions under which the child shall be conceived. . . ."

Moreover, woman shall further assert her power by refusing to

remain the passive instrument of sensual self-gratification on the part
of men. Birth Control, in philosophy and practice, is the destroyer of
that dualism of the old sexual code. It denies that the sole purpose of
sexual activity is procreation; it also denies that sex should be reduced
to the level of sensual lust, or that woman should permit herself to be
the instrument of its satisfaction. In increasing and differentiating her
love demands, woman must elevate sex into another sphere, whereby
it may subserve and enhance the possibility of individual and human
expression. Man will gain in this no less than woman; for in the age-
old enslavement of woman he has enslaved himself; and in the liberation of womankind, all of humanity will experience the joys of a
new and fuller freedom.

On this great fundamental and pivotal point new light has been
thrown by Lord Bertrand Dawson, the physician of the King of
England. In the remarkable and epoch-making address at the
Birmingham Church Congress (referred to in my introduction), he
spoke of the supreme morality of the mutual and reciprocal joy in the
most intimate relation between man and woman. Without this reciprocity there can be no civilization worthy of the name. Lord
Dawson suggested that there should be added to the clauses of marriage in the Prayer Book "the complete realization of the love of this
man and this woman one for another," and in support of his conten-
tion declared that sex love between husband and wife—apart from
parenthood—was something to prize and cherish for its own sake.
The Lambeth Conference, he remarked, "envisaged a love inverte-
brate and joyless," whereas, in his view, natural passion in wedlock
was not a thing to be ashamed of or unduly repressed. The pro-
nouncement of the Church of England, as set forth in Resolution 68
of the Lambeth Conference seems to imply condemnation of sex love
as such, and to imply sanction of sex love only as a means to an
end,—namely, procreation. The Lambeth Resolution stated:

"In opposition to the teaching which under the name of science
and religion encourages married people in the deliberate cultivation
of sexual union as an end in itself, we steadfastly uphold what must
always be regarded as the governing considerations of Christian marriage. One is the primary purpose for which marriage exists—namely,
the continuation of the race through the gift and heritage of children;
the other is the paramount importance in married life of deliberate
and thoughtful self-control."

In answer to this point of view Lord Dawson asserted:

"Sex love has, apart from parenthood, a purport of its own. It is
something to prize and to cherish for its own sake. It is an essential
part of health and happiness in marriage. And now, if you will allow

me, I will carry this argument a step further. If sexual union is a gift of God it is worth learning how to use it. Within its own sphere it should be cultivated so as to bring physical satisfaction to both, not merely to one. . . . The real problems before us are those of sex love and child love; and by sex love I mean that love which involves intercourse or the desire for such. It is necessary to my argument to emphasize that sex love is one of the dominating forces of the world. Not only does history show the destinies of nations and dynasties determined by its sway—but here in our every-day life we see its influence, direct or indirect, forceful and ubiquitous beyond aught else. Any statesmanlike view, therefore, will recognize that here we have an instinct so fundamental, so imperious, that its influence is a fact which has to be accepted; suppress it you cannot. You may guide it into healthy channels, but an outlet it will have, and if that outlet is inadequate and unduly obstructed irregular channels will be forced. . . .

"The attainment of mutual and reciprocal joy in their relations constitutes a firm bond between two people, and makes for durability of the marriage tie. Reciprocity in sex love is the physical counterpart of sympathy. More marriages fail from inadequate and clumsy sex love than from too much sex love. The lack of proper understanding is in no small measure responsible for the unfulfilment of connubial happiness, and every degree of discontent and unhappiness may, from this cause, occur, leading to rupture of the marriage bond itself. How often do medical men have to deal with these difficulties, and how fortunate if such difficulties are disclosed early enough in married life to be rectified. Otherwise how tragic may be their consequences, and many a case in the Divorce Court has thus had its origin. To the foregoing contentions, it might be objected, you are encouraging passion. My reply would be, passion is a worthy possession—most men, who are any good, are capable of passion. You all enjoy ardent and passionate love in art and literature. Why not give it a place in real life? Why some people look askance at passion is because they are confusing it with sensuality. Sex love without passion is a poor, lifeless thing. Sensuality, on the other hand, is on a level with gluttony—a physical excess—detached from sentiment, chivalry, or tenderness. It is just as important to give sex love its place as to avoid its over-emphasis. Its real and effective restraints are those imposed by a loving and sympathetic companionship, by the privileges of parenthood, the exacting claims of career and that civic sense which prompts men to do social service. Now that the revision of the Prayer Book is receiving consideration, I should like to suggest with great respect an addition made to the objects of marriage in the Marriage Service, in these terms, 'The complete realization of the love of this man and this woman, the one for the other.'"

Turning to the specific problem of Birth Control, Lord Dawson declared, "that Birth Control is here to stay. It is an established fact, and for good or evil has to be accepted. Although the extent of its application can be and is being modified, no denunciations will abolish it. Despite the influence and condemnations of the Church, it has been practised in France for well over half a century, and in Belgium and other Roman Catholic countries is extending. And if the Roman Catholic Church, with its compact organization, its power of authority and its disciplines, cannot check this procedure, it is not likely that Protestant Churches will be able to do so, for Protestant religions depend for their strength on the conviction and esteem they establish in the heads and hearts of their people. The reasons which lead parents to limit their offspring are sometimes selfish, but more often honorable and cogent."

A report of the Fabian Society on the morality of Birth Control, based upon a census conducted under the chairmanship of Sidney Webb, concludes: "These facts—which we are bound to face whether we like them or not—will appear in different lights to different people. In some quarters it seems to be sufficient to dismiss them with moral indignation, real or simulated. Such a judgment appears both irrelevant and futile. . . . If a course of conduct is habitually and deliberately pursued by vast multitudes of otherwise well-conducted people, forming probably a majority of the whole educated class of the nation, we must assume that it does not conflict with their actual code of morality. They may be intellectually mistaken, but they are not doing what they feel to be wrong."

The moral justification and ethical necessity of Birth Control need not be empirically based upon the mere approval of experience and custom. Its morality is more profound. Birth Control is an ethical necessity for humanity to-day because it places in our hands a new instrument of self-expression and self-realization. It gives us control over one of the primordial forces of nature, to which in the past the majority of mankind have been enslaved, and by which it has been cheapened and debased. It arouses us to the possibility of newer and greater freedom. It develops the power, the responsibility and intelligence to use this freedom in living a liberated and abundant life. It permits us to enjoy this liberty without danger of infringing upon the similar liberty of our fellow men, or of injuring and curtailing the freedom of the next generation. It shows us that we need not seek in the amassing of worldly wealth, nor in the illusion of some extraterrestrial Heaven or earthly Utopia of a remote future the road to human development. The Kingdom of Heaven is in a very definite sense within us. Not by leaving our body and our fundamental humanity behind us, not by aiming to be anything but what we are, shall we become ennobled or immortal. By knowing ourselves, by expressing ourselves, by realizing ourselves more completely than has ever before been possible, not only shall we attain the kingdom ourselves but we shall hand on the torch of life undimmed to our children and the children of our children.

Mary McLeod Bethune

(1875–1955)

A CENTURY OF PROGRESS OF NEGRO WOMEN
June 30, 1933

*Born the daughter of former slaves, Mary McLeod Bethune is best re-
membered as the founder of the Daytona Normal and Industrial Institute
for Negro Girls, which is now known as Bethune-Cookman College in
Daytona Beach, Florida. An energetic leader of numerous civil rights
organizations, Bethune was eventually named by Franklin D. Roosevelt
as the director of the Office of Minority Affairs in the National Youth
Administration in 1935. The speech that follows was delivered on June
30, 1933, before the Chicago Women's Federation.*

To FREDERICK DOUGLASS is credited the plea that, "the Negro be
not judged by the heights to which he is risen, but by the depths from
which he has climbed." Judged on that basis, the Negro woman embodies one of the modern miracles of the New World.

One hundred years ago she was the most pathetic figure on the
American continent. She was not a person, in the opinion of many,
but a thing—a thing whose personality had no claim to the respect of
mankind. She was a household drudge,—a means for getting distasteful work done; she was an animated agricultural implement to aug-
ment the service of mules and plows in cultivating and harvesting the
cotton crop. Then she was an automatic incubator, a producer of
human live stock, beneath whose heart and lungs more potential laborers could be bred and nurtured and brought to the light of toil-
some day.

Today she stands side by side with the finest manhood the race has
been able to produce. Whatever the achievements of the Negro man
in letters, business, art, pulpit, civic progress and moral reform, he
cannot but share them with his sister of darker hue. Whatever glory

belongs to the race for a development unprecedented in history for the given length of time, a full share belongs to the womanhood of the race.

By the very force of circumstances, the part she has played in the progress of the race has been of necessity, to a certain extent, subtle and indirect. She has not always been permitted a place in the front ranks where she could show her face and make her voice heard with effect. But she has been quick to seize every opportunity which presented itself to come more and more into the open and strive directly for the uplift of the race and nation. In that direction, her achievements have been amazing.

Negro women have made outstanding contributions in the arts. Meta V. W. Fuller and May Howard Jackson are significant figures in Fine Arts development. Angelina Grimke, Georgia Douglass Johnson and Alice Dunbar Nelson are poets of note. Jessie Fausett has become famous as a novelist. In the field of Music Anita Patti Brown, Lillian Evanti, Elizabeth Greenfield, Florence Cole-Talbert, Marion Anderson and Marie Selika stand out pre-eminently.

Very early in the post-emancipation period women began to show signs of ability to contribute to the business progress of the Race. Maggie L. Walker, who is outstanding as the guiding spirit of the Order of Saint Luke, in 1902 went before her Grand Council with a plan for a Saint Luke Penny Savings Bank. This organization started with a deposit of about eight thousand dollars and twenty-five thousand in paid-up capital, with Maggie L. Walker as the first Woman Bank President in America. For twenty-seven years she has held this place. Her bank has paid dividends to its stockholders; has served as a depository for gas and water accounts of the city of Richmond and has given employment to hundreds of Negro clerks, bookkeepers and office workers.

With America's great emphasis on the physical appearance, a Negro woman left her washtub and ventured into the field of facial beautification. From a humble beginning Madame C. J. Walker built a substantial institution that is a credit to American business in every way.

Mrs. Annie M. Malone is another pioneer in this field of successful business. The C. J. Walker Manufacturing Company and the Poro College do not confine their activities in the field of beautification to race. They serve both races and give employment to both.

When the ballot was made available to the Womanhood of America, the sister of darker hue was not slow to seize the advantage. In sections where the Negro could gain access to the voting booth, the intelligent, forward-looking element of the Race's women have taken hold of political issues with an enthusiasm and mental acumen that might well set worthy examples for other groups. Oftimes she has led the struggle toward moral improvement and political record, and has compelled her reluctant brother to follow her determined lead.

In time of war as in time of peace, the Negro woman has ever been ready to serve for her people's and the nation's good. During the recent World War she pleaded to go in the uniform of the Red Cross nurse and was denied the opportunity only on the basis of racial distinction.

Addie W. Hunton and Kathryn M. Johnson gave yeoman service with the American Expeditionary Forces with the Y.M.C.A. group.

Negro women have thrown themselves whole-heartedly into the organization of groups to direct the social uplift of their fellowmen, one of the greatest achievements of the race.

Perhaps the most outstanding individual social worker of our group today is Jane E. Hunter, founder and executive secretary of the Phillis Wheatley Association, Cleveland, Ohio.

In November, 1911, Miss Hunter, who had been a nurse in Cleveland for only a short time, recognizing the need for a Working Girls' Home, organized the Association and prepared to establish the work. Today the Association is housed in a magnificent structure of nine stories, containing one hundred thirty-five rooms, offices, parlours, a cafeteria and beauty parlour. It is not only a home for working girls but a recreational center and ideal hospice for the young Negro woman who is living away from home. It maintains an employment department and a fine, up-to-date camp. Branches of the activities of the main Phillis Wheatley are located in other sections of Cleveland, special emphasis being given to the recreational facilities for children and young women of the vicinities in which the branches are located.

In no field of modern social relationship has the hand of service and the influence of the Negro woman been felt more distinctly than in the Negro orthodox church. It may be safely said that the chief sustaining force in support of the pulpit and the various phases of missionary enterprise has been the feminine element of the membership. The development of the Negro church since the Civil War has been another of the modern miracles. Throughout its growth the untiring effort, the unflagging enthusiasm, the sacrificial contribution of time, effort and cash earnings of the black woman have been the most significant factors, without which the modern Negro church would have no history worth the writing.

Both before and since emancipation, by some rare gift, she has been able to hold onto the fibres of family unity and keep the home one unimpaired whole. In recent years it has become increasingly the case where in many instances, the mother is the sole dependence of the home, and single-handed, fights the wolf from the door, while the father submits unwillingly to enforced idleness and unavoidable unemployment. Yet in myriads of instances she controls home discipline with a tight rein and exerts a unifying influence that is the miracle of the century.

The true worth of a race must be measured by the character of its womanhood.

As the years have gone on the Negro woman has touched the most vital fields in the civilization of today. Wherever she has contributed she has left the mark of a strong character. The educational institutions she has established and directed have met the needs of her young people; her cultural development has concentrated itself into artistic presentation accepted and acclaimed by meritorious critics; she is successful as a poet and a novelist; she is shrewd in business and capable in politics; she recognizes the importance of uplifting her people through social, civic and religious activities; starting at the time when as a "mammy" she nursed the infants of the other race and taught him her meagre store of truth, she has been a contributing factor of note to interracial relations. Finally, through the past century she has made and kept her home intact—humble though it may have been in many instances. She has made and is making history.

Eleanor Roosevelt

(1884–1962)

ON THE ADOPTION OF THE UNIVERSAL DECLARATION OF HUMAN RIGHTS

December 9, 1948

Anna Eleanor Roosevelt served as First Lady of the United States from 1933–1945, during which time she used her influence to support her husband's New Deal policies, while advocating for civil rights and women's suffrage. Her great work for human rights around the world led Harry Truman to call her "First Lady of the World." This impassioned and historic speech was delivered before the United Nations General Assembly on December 9, 1948.

MR. PRESIDENT, FELLOW DELEGATES:

The long and meticulous study and debate of which this Universal Declaration of Human Rights is the product means that it reflects the composite views of the many men and governments who have contributed to its formulation. Not every man nor every government can have what he wants in a document of this kind. There are of course particular provisions in the Declaration before us with which we are not fully satisfied. I have no doubt this is true of other delegations, and it would still be true if we continued our labors over many years. Taken as a whole the Delegation of the United States believes that this is a good document—even a great document—and we propose to give it our full support. The position of the United States on the various parts of the Declaration is a matter of record in the Third Committee. I shall not burden the Assembly, and particularly my colleagues of the Third Committee, with a restatement of that position here.

I should like to comment briefly on the amendments proposed by the Soviet delegation. The language of these amendments has been dressed up somewhat, but the substance is the same as the amendments which were offered by the Soviet delegation in committee and

rejected after exhaustive discussion. Substantially the same amendments have been previously considered and rejected in the Human
Rights Commission. We in the United States admire those who fight
for their convictions, and the Soviet delegation has fought for their
convictions. But in the older democracies we have learned that sometimes we bow to the will of the majority. In doing that, we do not
give up our convictions. We continue sometimes to persuade, and
eventually we may be successful. But we know that we have to work
together and we have to progress. So, we believe that when we have
made a good fight, and the majority is against us, it is perhaps better
tactics to try to cooperate.

I feel bound to say that I think perhaps it is somewhat of an impo-
sition on this Assembly to have these amendments offered again here,
and I am confident that they will be rejected without debate.

The first two paragraphs of the amendment to article 3 deal with
the question of minorities, which committee 3 decided required further study, and has recommended, in a separate resolution, their reference to the Economic and Social Council and the Human Rights
Commission. As set out in the Soviet amendment, this provision
clearly states "group," and not "individual," rights.

The Soviet amendment to article 20 is obviously a very restrictive
statement of the right to freedom of opinion and expression. It sets up
standards which would enable any state practically to deny all freedom
of opinion and expression without violating the article. It introduces
the terms "democratic view," "democratic systems," "democratic
state," and "fascism," which we know all too well from debates in this
Assembly over the past two years on warmongering and related subjects are liable to the most flagrant abuse and diverse interpretations.

The statement of the Soviet delegate here tonight is a very good case
in point on this. The Soviet amendment of article 22 introduces new
elements into the article without improving the committed text and
again introduces specific reference to "discrimination." As was repeatedly
pointed out in committee 3, the question of discrimination is compre-
hensively covered in article 2 of the Declaration, so that its restatement
elsewhere is completely unnecessary and also has the effect of weakening
the comprehensive principles stated in article 2. The new article proposed by the Soviet delegation is but a restatement of State obligation,
which the Soviet delegation attempted to introduce into practically every
article in the Declaration. It would convert the Declaration into a document stating obligations on states, thereby changing completely its character as a statement of principles to serve as a common standard of
achievement for the members of the United Nations.

The Soviet proposal for deferring consideration of the Declaration to the 4th session of the Assembly requires no comment. An identical text was rejected in committee 3 by a vote of 6 in favor and 26 against. We are all agreed, I am sure, that the Declaration, which has been worked on with such great effort and devotion, and over such a long period of time, must be approved by this Assembly at this session.

Certain provisions of the Declaration are stated in such broad terms as to be acceptable only because of the provisions in article 30 providing for limitation on the exercise of the rights for the purpose of meeting the requirements of morality, public order, and the general welfare. An example of this is the provision that everyone has the right to equal access to the public service in his country. The basic principle of equality and of nondiscrimination as to public employment is sound, but it cannot be accepted without limitation. My government, for example, would consider that this is unquestionably subject to limitation in the interest of public order and the general welfare. It would not consider that the exclusion from public employment of persons holding subversive political beliefs and not loyal to the basic principles and practices of the constitution and laws of the country would in any way infringe upon this right.

Likewise, my government has made it clear in the course of the development of the Declaration that it does not consider that the economic and social and cultural rights stated in the Declaration imply an obligation on governments to assure the enjoyment of these rights by direct governmental action. This was made quite clear in the Human Rights Commission text of article 23 which served as a so-called "umbrella" article to the articles on economic and social rights. We consider that the principle has not been affected by the fact that this article no longer contains a reference to the articles which follow it. This in no way affects our whole-hearted support for the basic principles of economic, social, and cultural rights set forth in these articles.

In giving our approval to the Declaration today it is of primary importance that we keep clearly in mind the basic character of the document. It is not a treaty; it is not an international agreement. It is not and does not purport to be a statement of law or of legal obligation. It is a Declaration of basic principles of human rights and freedoms, to be stamped with the approval of the General Assembly by formal vote of its members, and to serve as a common standard of achievement for all peoples of all nations.

We stand today at the threshold of a great event both in the life of the United Nations and in the life of mankind. This Universal Declaration of Human Rights may well become the international Magna Carta of all men everywhere. We hope its proclamation by the General Assembly will be an event comparable to the proclamation of the Declaration of the Rights of Man by the French people in 1789, the adoption of the Bill of Rights by the people of the United States, and the adoption of comparable declarations at different times in other countries.

At a time when there are so many issues on which we find it difficult to reach a common basis of agreement, it is a significant fact that 58 states have found such a large measure of agreement in the complex field of human rights. This must be taken as testimony of our common aspiration first voiced in the Charter of the United Nations to lift men everywhere to a higher standard of life and to a greater enjoyment of freedom. Man's desire for peace lies behind this Declaration. The realization that the flagrant violation of human rights by Nazi and Fascist countries sowed the seeds of the last world war has supplied the impetus for the work which brings us to the moment of achievement here today.

In a recent speech in Canada, Gladstone Murray said:

> "The central fact is that man is fundamentally a moral being, that the light we have is imperfect does not matter so long as we are always trying to improve it ... we are equal in sharing the moral freedom that distinguishes us as men. Man's status makes each individual an end in himself. No man is by nature simply the servant of the state or of another man . . . the ideal and fact of freedom—and not technology—are the true distinguishing marks of our civilization."

This Declaration is based upon the spiritual fact that man must have freedom in which to develop his full stature and through common effort to raise the level of human dignity. We have much to do to fully achieve and to assure the rights set forth in this Declaration. But having them put before us with the moral backing of 58 nations will be a great step forward.

As we here bring to fruition our labors on this Declaration of Human Rights, we must at the same time rededicate ourselves to the unfinished task which lies before us. We can now move on with new courage and inspiration to the completion of an international covenant on human rights and of measures for the implementation of human rights.

In conclusion, I feel that I cannot do better than to repeat the call to action by Secretary Marshall in his opening statement to this Assembly:

> "Let this third regular session of the General Assembly approve by an overwhelming majority the Declaration of Human Rights as a standard of conduct for all; and let us, as Members of the United Nations, conscious of our own short-comings and imperfections, join our effort in good faith to live up to this high standard."

Margaret Chase Smith

(1897–1995)

DECLARATION OF CONSCIENCE
June 1, 1950

Margaret Chase Smith was the first woman ever to be elected to both houses of the United States Congress. Elected into the Seventy-Sixth Congress in 1940, Smith served in the House of Representatives for Maine's 2nd district for eight years, after which she served four consecutive terms representing Maine in the Senate, before losing her reelection bid in 1972. The following address was delivered before the United States Senate on June 1, 1950.

MR. PRESIDENT:

I would like to speak briefly and simply about a serious national condition. It is a national feeling of fear and frustration that could result in national suicide and the end of everything that we Americans hold dear. It is a condition that comes from the lack of effective leadership in either the Legislative Branch or the Executive Branch of our Government.

That leadership is so lacking that serious and responsible proposals are being made that national advisory commissions be appointed to provide such critically needed leadership.

I speak as briefly as possible because too much harm has already been done with irresponsible words of bitterness and selfish political opportunism. I speak as briefly as possible because the issue is too great to be obscured by eloquence. I speak simply and briefly in the hope that my words will be taken to heart.

I speak as a Republican. I speak as a woman. I speak as a United States Senator. I speak as an American.

The United States Senate has long enjoyed worldwide respect as the greatest deliberative body in the world. But recently that deliberative character has too often been debased to the level of a forum of hate and character assassination sheltered by the shield of congressional immunity.

It is ironical that we Senators can in debate in the Senate directly or indirectly, by any form of words, impute to any American who is not a Senator any conduct or motive unworthy or unbecoming an American—and without that non-Senator American having any legal redress against us—yet if we say the same thing in the Senate about our colleagues we can be stopped on the grounds of being out of order.

It is strange that we can verbally attack anyone else without restraint and with full protection and yet we hold ourselves above the same type of criticism here on the Senate Floor. Surely the United States Senate is big enough to take self-criticism and self-appraisal. Surely we should be able to take the same kind of character attacks that we "dish out" to outsiders.

I think that it is high time for the United States Senate and its members to do some soul-searching—for us to weigh our consciences—on the manner in which we are performing our duty to the people of America—on the manner in which we are using or abusing our individual powers and privileges.

I think that it is high time that we remembered that we have sworn to uphold and defend the Constitution. I think that it is high time that we remembered that the Constitution, as amended, speaks not only of the freedom of speech but also of trial by jury instead of trial by accusation.

Whether it be a criminal prosecution in court or a character prosecution in the Senate, there is little practical distinction when the life of a person has been ruined.

Those of us who shout the loudest about Americanism in making character assassinations are all too frequently those who, by our own words and acts, ignore some of the basic principles of Americanism:

> The right to criticize;
> The right to hold unpopular beliefs;
> The right to protest;
> The right of independent thought.

The exercise of these rights should not cost one single American citizen his reputation or his right to a livelihood nor should he be in danger of losing his reputation or livelihood merely because he happens to know someone who holds unpopular beliefs. Who of us doesn't? Otherwise none of us could call our souls our own. Otherwise thought control would have set in.

The American people are sick and tired of being afraid to speak their minds lest they be politically smeared as "Communists" or "Fascists" by their opponents. Freedom of speech is not what it used to be in America. It has been so abused by some that it is not exercised by others.

The American people are sick and tired of seeing innocent people smeared and guilty people whitewashed. But there have been enough proved cases such as the Amerasia case, the Hiss case, the Coplon case, the Gold case, to cause nationwide distrust and strong suspicion that there may be something to the unproved, sensational accusations.

As a Republican, I say to my colleagues on this side of the aisle that the Republican Party faces a challenge today that is not unlike the challenge that it faced back in Lincoln's day. The Republican Party so successfully met that challenge that it emerged from the Civil War as the champion of a united nation—in addition to being a Party that unrelentingly fought loose spending and loose programs.

Today our country is being psychologically divided by the confusion and the suspicions that are bred in the United States Senate to spread like cancerous tentacles of "know nothing, suspect everything" attitudes. Today we have a Democratic Administration that has developed a mania for loose spending and loose programs. History is repeating itself—and the Republican Party again has the opportunity to emerge as the champion of unity and prudence.

The record of the present Democratic Administration has provided us with sufficient campaign issues without the necessity of resorting to political smears. America is rapidly losing its position as leader of the world simply because the Democratic Administration has pitifully failed to provide effective leadership.

The Democratic Administration has completely confused the American people by its daily contradictory grave warnings and optimistic assurances—that show the people that our Democratic Administration has no idea of where it is going.

The Democratic Administration has greatly lost the confidence of the American people by its complacency to the threat of communism here at home and the leak of vital secrets to Russia through key officials of the Democratic Administration. There are enough proved cases to make this point without diluting our criticism with unproved charges.

Surely these are sufficient reasons to make it clear to the American people that it is time for a change and that a Republican victory is necessary to the security of this country. Surely it is clear that this nation will continue to suffer as long as it is governed by the present ineffective Democratic Administration.

Yet to displace it with a Republican regime embracing a philosophy that lacks political integrity or intellectual honesty would prove equally disastrous to this nation. The nation sorely needs a Republican victory. But I don't want to see the Republican Party ride to political victory on the Four Horsemen of Calumny—Fear, Ignorance, Bigotry, and Smear.

I doubt if the Republican Party could—simply because I don't believe the American people will uphold any political party that puts political exploitation above national interest. Surely we Republicans aren't that desperate for victory.

I don't want to see the Republican Party win that way. While it might be a fleeting victory for the Republican Party, it would be a more lasting defeat for the American people. Surely it would ultimately be suicide for the Republican Party and the two-party system that has protected our American liberties from the dictatorship of a one-party system.

As members of the Minority Party, we do not have the primary authority to formulate the policy of our Government. But we do have the responsibility of rendering constructive criticism, of clarifying issues, of allaying fears by acting as responsible citizens.

As a woman, I wonder how the mothers, wives, sisters, and daughters feel about the way in which members of their families have been politically mangled in Senate debate and I use the word "debate" advisedly

As a United States Senator, I am not proud of the way in which the Senate has been made a publicity platform for irresponsible sensationalism. I am not proud of the reckless abandon in which unproved charges have been hurled from the side of the aisle. I am not proud of the obviously staged, undignified countercharges that have been attempted in retaliation from the other side of the aisle.

I don't like the way the Senate has been made a rendezvous for vilification, for selfish political gain at the sacrifice of individual reputations and national unity. I am not proud of the way we smear outsiders from the Floor of the Senate and hide behind the cloak of congressional immunity and still place ourselves beyond criticism on the Floor of the Senate.

As an American, I am shocked at the way Republicans and Democrats alike are playing directly into the Communist design of "confuse, divide, and conquer." As an American, I don't want a Democratic Administration "whitewash" or "cover-up" any more than I want a Republican smear or witch hunt.

As an American, I condemn a Republican "Fascist" just as much as I condemn a Democratic "Communist." I condemn a Democrat

"Fascist" just as much as I condemn a Republican "Communist." They are equally dangerous to you and me and to our country. As an American, I want to see our nation recapture the strength and unity it once had when we fought the enemy instead of ourselves.

It is with these thoughts that I have drafted what I call a "Declaration of Conscience." I am gratified that Senator Tobey, Senator Aiken, Senator Morse, Senator Ives, Senator Thye, and Senator Hendrickson have concurred in that declaration and have authorized me to announce their concurrence.

Shirley Chisholm

(1924–2005)

PEOPLE AND PEACE, NOT PROFITS AND WAR
March 16, 1969

Shirley Chisholm became the first African-American woman elected to the U.S. Congress in 1968, when she defeated James Farmer in the race to represent New York's Twelfth Congressional District. The following speech, delivered on the floor of the U.S. House of Representatives on March 16, 1969, challenges Congress to pay as much attention to the nation's poor and needy as it does on developing "elaborate" and "impractical" military weapons systems.

MR. SPEAKER, on the same day President Nixon announced he had decided the United States will not be safe unless we start to build a defense system against missiles, the Head Start program in the District of Columbia was cut back for the lack of money.

As a teacher, and as a woman, I do not think I will ever understand what kind of values can be involved in spending $9 billion—and more, I am sure—on elaborate, unnecessary, and impractical weapons when several thousand disadvantaged children in the nation's capital get nothing.

When the new administration took office, I was one of the many Americans who hoped it would mean that our country would benefit from the fresh perspectives, the new ideas, the different priorities of a leader who had no part in the mistakes of the past. Mr. Nixon had said things like this: "If our cities are to be livable for the next generation, we can delay no longer in launching new approaches to the problems that beset them and to the tensions that tear them apart." And he said, "When you cut expenditures for education, what you are doing is shortchanging the American future."

But frankly, I have never cared too much what people say. What

I am interested in is what they do. We I have waited to see what the new administration is going to do. The pattern is now becoming clear. Apparently launching those new programs can be delayed for a while, after all. It seems we have to get some missiles launched first. Recently the new secretary of commerce spelled it out. The secretary, Mr. Stans, told a reporter that the new administration is "pretty well agreed it must take time out from major social objectives" until it can stop inflation.

The new secretary of health, education, and welfare, Robert Finch, came to the Hill to tell the House Education and Labor Committee that he thinks we should spend more on education, particularly in city schools. But, he said, unfortunately we cannot "afford" to, until we have reached some kind of honorable solution to the Vietnam War. I was glad to read that the distinguished Member from Oregon [Mrs. Green] asked Mr. Finch this: "With the crisis we have in education, and the crisis in our cities, can we wait to settle the war? Shouldn't it be the other way around? Unless we can meet the crisis in education, we really can't afford the war."

Secretary of Defense Melvin Laird came to Capitol Hill, too. His mission was to sell the antiballistic missile insanity to the Senate. He was asked what the new administration is doing about the war. To hear him, one would have thought it was 1968, that the former secretary of state was defending the former policies, that nothing had ever happened, a president had never decided not to run because he knew the nation would reject him in despair over this tragic war we have blundered into. Mr. Laird talked to being prepared to spend at least two more years in Vietnam.

Two more years. Two more years of hunger for Americans, of death for our best young men, of children here at home suffering the lifelong handicap of not having a good education when they are young. Two more years of high taxes collected to feed the cancerous growth of a Defense Department budget that now consumes two-thirds of our federal income.

Two more years of too little being done to fight our greatest enemies—poverty, prejudice, and neglect—here in our own country. Two more years of fantastic waste in the Defense Department and of penny pinching on social programs. Our country cannot survive two more years, or four, of these kinds of policies. It must stop this year—now.

Now, I am not a pacifist. I am deeply, unalterably opposed to this war in Vietnam. Apart from all other considerations—and they are many—the main fact is that we cannot squander the lives, the money, the energy that we need desperately here, in our cities, in our schools.

I wonder whether we cannot reverse our whole approach to spending. For years, we have given the military, the defense industry, a blank check. New weapons systems are dreamed up, billions are spent, and many times they are found to be impractical, inefficient, unsatisfactory, even worthless. What do we do then? We spend more money on them. But with social programs, what do we do? Take the Job Corps. Its failure has been mercilessly exposed and criticized. If it had been a military research and development project, they would have been covered up or explained away, and Congress would have been ready to pour more billions after those that had been wasted on it.

The case of Pride, Inc., is interesting. This vigorous, successful black organization here in Washington, conceived and built by young, inner-city men, has been ruthlessly attacked by its enemies in the government, in this Congress. At least six auditors from the General Accounting Office were put to work investigating Pride. They worked seven months and spent more than $100,000. They uncovered a fraud. It was something less than $2,100. Meanwhile, millions of dollars—billions of dollars, in fact—were being spent by the Department of Defense, and how many auditors and investigators were checking into their negotiated contracts? Five.

We Americans have come to feel that it is our mission to make the world free. We believe that we are the good guys everywhere—in Vietnam, in Latin America, wherever we go. We believe that we are the good guys at home, too. When the Kerner Commission told white America what black America had always known, that prejudice and hatred built the nation's slums, maintain them, and profit by them, white America would not believe it. But it is true. Unless we start to fight and defeat the enemies of poverty and racism in our own country and make our talk of equality and opportunity ring true, we are exposed as hypocrites in the eyes of the world when we talk about making other people free.

I am deeply disappointed at the clear evidence that the number-one priority of the new administration is to buy more and more weapons of war, to return to the era of the Cold War, to ignore the war we must fight here—the war that is not optional. There is only one way, I believe, to turn these policies around. The Congress can respond to the mandate that the American people have clearly expressed. They have said, "End this war. Stop the waste. Stop the killing. Do something for your own people first." We must find the money to "launch the new approaches," as Mr. Nixon said. We must force the administration to rethink its distorted, unreal scale of priorities. Our children, our jobless men, our deprived, rejected, and starving fellow citizens must come first.

For this reason, I intend to vote "No" on every money bill that comes to the floor of this House that provides any funds for the Department of Defense—any bill whatsoever—until the time comes when our values and priorities have been turned rightside up again, until the monstrous waste and the shocking profits in the defense budget have been eliminated and our country starts to use its strength, its tremendous resources, for people and peace, not for profits and war.

It was Calvin Coolidge, I believe, who made the comment that "the business of America is business." We are now spending $80 billion a year on defense. That is two-thirds of every tax dollar. At this time, gentlemen, the business of America is war, and it is time for a change.

Geraldine Ferraro

(b. 1935)

VICE PRESIDENTIAL NOMINATION
ACCEPTANCE ADDRESS
July 19, 1984

Geraldine Anne Ferraro is best known as the first woman candidate for vice president ever to run on a national party ticket, running alongside Walter Mondale in the 1984 presidential election. Prior to 1984, Ferraro earned her reputation as a staunch advocate for social justice during her tenures both in the Queens County District Attorney's Office, and as the congresswoman for New York's Ninth District in the U.S. House of Representatives. The following speech was delivered on July 19, 1984, upon Ferraro's nomination for vice president of the United States.

LADIES AND GENTLEMEN OF THE CONVENTION:

My name is Geraldine Ferraro. I stand before you to proclaim tonight: America is the land where dreams can come true for all of us. As I stand before the American people and think of the honor this great convention has bestowed upon me, I recall the words of Dr. Martin Luther King Jr., who made America stronger by making America more free. He said, "Occasionally in life there are moments which cannot be completely explained by words. Their meaning can only be articulated by the inaudible language of the heart." Tonight is such a moment for me.

My heart is filled with pride. My fellow citizens, I proudly accept your nomination for Vice President of the United States.

And I am proud to run with a man who will be one of the great Presidents of this century, Walter F. Mondale. Tonight, the daughter of a woman whose highest goal was a future for her children talks to our nation's oldest party about a future for us all. Tonight, the daughter of working Americans tells all Americans that the future is within our reach, if we're willing to reach for it. Tonight, the daughter of an immigrant from Italy has been chosen to run for [Vice] President in the new land my father came to love.

Our faith that we can shape a better future is what the American dream is all about. The promise of our country is that the rules are fair. If you work hard and play by the rules, you can earn your share of America's blessings. Those are the beliefs I learned from my parents. And those are the values I taught my students as a teacher in the public schools of New York City.

At night, I went to law school. I became an assistant district attorney, and I put my share of criminals behind bars. I believe if you obey the law, you should be protected. But if you break the law, you must pay for your crime.

When I first ran for Congress, all the political experts said a Democrat could not win my home district in Queens. I put my faith in the people and the values that we shared. Together, we proved the political experts wrong. In this campaign, Fritz Mondale and I have put our faith in the people. And we are going to prove the experts wrong again. We are going to win. We are going to win because Americans across this country believe in the same basic dream.

Last week, I visited Elmore, Minnesota, the small town where Fritz Mondale was raised. And soon Fritz and Joan will visit our family in Queens. Nine hundred people live in Elmore. In Queens, there are 2,000 people on one block. You would think we'd be different, but we're not. Children walk to school in Elmore past grain elevators; in Queens, they pass by subway stops. But, no matter where they live, their future depends on education, and their parents are willing to do their part to make those schools as good as they can be. In Elmore, there are family farms; in Queens, small businesses. But the men and women who run them all take pride in supporting their families through hard work and initiative. On the 4th of July in Elmore, they hang flags out on Main Street; in Queens, they fly them over Grand Avenue. But all of us love our country, and stand ready to defend the freedom that it represents.

Americans want to live by the same set of rules. But under this administration, the rules are rigged against too many of our people. It isn't right that every year the share of taxes paid by individual citizens is going up, while the share paid by large corporations is getting smaller and smaller. The rules say: Everyone in our society should contribute their fair share. It isn't right that this year Ronald Reagan will hand the American people a bill for interest on the national debt larger than the entire cost of the federal government under John F.

Kennedy. Our parents left us a growing economy. The rules say: We must not leave our kids a mountain of debt.

It isn't right that a woman should get paid 59 cents on the dollar for the same work as a man.

If you play by the rules, you deserve a fair day's pay for a fair day's work. It isn't right that, if trends continue, by the year 2000 nearly all of the poor people in America will be women and children. The rules of a decent society say: When you distribute sacrifice in times of austerity, you don't put women and children first. It isn't right that young people today fear they won't get the Social Security they paid for, and that older Americans fear that they will lose what they have already learned [earned]. Social Security is a contract between the last generation and the next, and the rules say: You don't break contracts.

We are going to keep faith with older Americans. We hammered out a fair compromise in the Congress to save Social Security. Every group sacrificed to keep the system sound. It is time Ronald Reagan stopped scaring our senior citizens.

It isn't right that young couples question whether to bring children into a world of 50,000 nuclear warheads. That isn't the vision for which Americans have struggled for more than two centuries. And our future doesn't have to be that way. Change is in the air, just as surely as when John Kennedy beckoned America to a new frontier; when Sally Ride rocketed into space; and when Reverend Jesse Jackson ran for the office of President of the United States.

By choosing a woman to run for our nation's second highest office, you send a powerful signal to all Americans: There are no doors we cannot unlock. We will place no limits on achievement. If we can do this, we can do anything.

Tonight, we reclaim our dream. We're going to make the rules of American life work fairly for all Americans again. To an Administration that would have us debate all over again whether the Voting Rights Act should be renewed and whether segregated schools should be tax exempt, we say, Mr. President: Those debates are over. On the issue of civil rights, voting rights, and affirmative action for minorities, we must not go backwards. We must—and we will—move forward to open the doors of opportunity.

To those who understand that our country cannot prosper unless we draw on the talents of all Americans, we say: We will pass the Equal Rights Amendment.

The issue is not what America can do for women, but what women can do for America.

To the Americans who will lead our country into the 21st century, we say: We will not have a Supreme Court that turns the clock back to the 19th century.

To those concerned about the strength of American and family values, as I am, I say: We are going to restore those values—love, caring, partnership—by including, and not excluding, those whose beliefs differ from our own. Because our own faith is strong, we will fight to preserve the freedom of faith for others.

To those working Americans who fear that banks, utilities, and large special interests have a lock on the White House, we say: Join us; let's elect the people's President; and let's have government by and for the American people again.

To an Administration that would savage student loans and education at the dawn of a new technological age, we say: You fit the classic definition of a cynic; you know the price of everything, but the value of nothing.

To our students and their parents, we say: We will insist on the highest standards of excellence, because the jobs of the future require skilled minds. To young Americans who may be called to our country's service, we say: We know your generation will proudly answer our country's call, as each generation before you.

This past year, we remembered the bravery and sacrifice of Americans at Normandy. And we finally paid tribute—as we should have done years ago—to that unknown soldier who represents all the brave young Americans who died in Vietnam. Let no one doubt, we will defend America's security and the cause of freedom around the world. But we want a President who tells us what America's fighting for, not just what we are fighting against.

We want a President who will defend human rights, not just where it is convenient, but wherever freedom is at risk—from Chile to Afghanistan, from Poland to South Africa. To those who have watched this administration's confusion in the Middle East, as it has tilted first toward one and then another of Israel's long-time enemies and wonder: "Will America stand by her friends and sister democracy?" we say: America knows who her friends are in the Middle East and around the world. America will stand with Israel always.

Finally, we want a President who will keep America strong, but use that strength to keep America and the world at peace. A nuclear freeze is not a slogan: It is a tool for survival in the nuclear age. If we leave our children nothing else, let us leave them this Earth as we found it: whole and green and full of life.

I know in my heart that Walter Mondale will be that President.

A wise man once said, "Every one of us is given the gift of life, and what a strange gift it is. If it is preserved jealously and selfishly, it impoverishes and saddens. But if it is spent for others, it enriches and beautifies." My fellow Americans: We can debate policies and programs, but in the end what separates the two parties in this election campaign is whether we use the gift of life for others or only ourselves.

Tonight, my husband, John, and our three children are in this hall with me. To my daughters, Donna and Laura, and my son, John Junior, I say: My mother did not break faith with me, and I will not break faith with you.

To all the children of America, I say: The generation before ours kept faith with us, and like them, we will pass on to you a stronger, more just America.

Thank you.

Ann Richards

(1933–2006)

DEMOCRATIC NATIONAL CONVENTION
KEYNOTE ADDRESS
July 18, 1988

*Dorothy Ann Willis Richards began her career in politics when she be-
came the first female commissioner of Travis County, Texas, in 1976.
Over the next two decades, Richards went on to become the Texas state
treasurer, eventually serving as governor for the Lone Star State from
1991–1995. The following speech was delivered on July 19, 1988, at
the Democratic National Convention while Richards was still treasurer
of Texas.*

THANK YOU. THANK YOU. Thank you, very much.

Good evening, ladies and gentlemen. Buenas noches, mis amigos.

I'm delighted to be here with you this evening, because after listening to George Bush all these years, I figured you needed to know
what a real Texas accent sounds like.

Twelve years ago Barbara Jordan, another Texas woman, Barbara
made the keynote address to this convention, and two women in a
hundred and sixty years is about par for the course.

But if you give us a chance, we can perform. After all, Ginger
Rogers did everything that Fred Astaire did. She just did it backwards
and in high heels.

I want to announce to this Nation that in a little more than 100
days, the Reagan-Meese-Deaver-Nofziger-Poindexter-North-Wein-
berger-Watt-Gorsuch-Lavelle-Stockman-Haig-Bork-Noriega-
George Bush [era] will be over!

You know, tonight I feel a little like I did when I played basketball
in the 8th grade. I thought I looked real cute in my uniform. And
then I heard a boy yell from the bleachers, "Make that basket,

Birdlegs." And my greatest fear is that same guy is somewhere out there in the audience tonight, and he's going to cut me down to size, because where I grew up there really wasn't much tolerance for self-importance, people who put on airs.

I was born during the Depression in a little community just outside Waco, and I grew up listening to Franklin Roosevelt on the radio. Well, it was back then that I came to understand the small truths and the hardships that bind neighbors together. Those were real people with real problems and they had real dreams about getting out of the Depression. I can remember summer nights when we'd put down what we called the Baptist pallet, and we listened to the grown-ups talk. I can still hear the sound of the dominoes clicking on the marble slab my daddy had found for a tabletop. I can still hear the laughter of the men telling jokes you weren't supposed to hear—talkin' about how big that old buck deer was, laughin' about mama puttin' Clorox in the well when the frog fell in.

They talked about war and Washington and what this country needed. They talked straight talk. And it came from people who were living their lives as best they could. And that's what we're gonna do tonight. We're gonna tell how the cow ate the cabbage.

I got a letter last week from a young mother in Lorena, Texas, and I wanna read part of it to you. She writes,

> "Our worries go from pay day to pay day, just like millions of others. And we have two fairly decent incomes, but I worry how I'm going to pay the rising car insurance and food. I pray my kids don't have a growth spurt from August to December, so I don't have to buy new jeans. We buy clothes at the budget stores and we have them fray and fade and stretch in the first wash. We ponder and try to figure out how we're gonna pay for college and braces and tennis shoes. We don't take vacations and we don't go out to eat. Please don't think me ungrateful. We have jobs and a nice place to live, and we're healthy. We're the people you see every day in the grocery stores, and we obey the laws. We pay our taxes. We fly our flags on holidays and we plod along trying to make it better for ourselves and our children and our parents. We aren't vocal any more. I think maybe we're too tired. I believe that people like us are forgotten in America."

Well of course you believe you're forgotten, because you have been. This Republican Administration treats us as if we were pieces of a puzzle that can't fit together. They've tried to put us into compartments and separate us from each other. Their political theory is "divide and conquer." They've suggested time and time again that what is of interest to one group of Americans is not of interest to any one else. We've been isolated. We've been lumped into that sad phraseology called "special interests." They've told farmers that they were selfish, that they would drive up food prices if they asked the government to intervene on behalf of the family farm, and we watched farms go on the auction block while we bought food from foreign countries. Well, that's wrong!

They told working mothers it's all their fault—their families are falling apart because they had to go to work to keep their kids in jeans and tennis shoes and college. And they're wrong! They told American labor they were trying to ruin free enterprise by asking for 60 days' notice of plant closings, and that's wrong. And they told the auto industry and the steel industry and the timber industry and the oil industry, companies being threatened by foreign products flooding this country, that you're "protectionist" if you think the government should enforce our trade laws. And that is wrong. When they belittle us for demanding clean air and clean water for trying to save the oceans and the ozone layer, that's wrong.

No wonder we feel isolated and confused. We want answers and their answer is that "something is wrong with you." Well nothing's wrong with you. Nothing's wrong with you that you can't fix in November!

We've been told—We've been told that the interests of the South and the Southwest are not the same interests as the North and the Northeast. They pit one group against the other. They've divided this country and in our isolation we think government isn't gonna help us, and we're alone in our feelings. We feel forgotten. Well, the fact is that we are not an isolated piece of their puzzle. We are one nation. We are the United States of America.

Now we Democrats believe that America is still the country of fair play, that we can come out of a small town or a poor neighborhood and have the same chance as anyone else; and it doesn't matter whether we are black or Hispanic or disabled or a women [sic]. We believe that America is a country where small business owners must succeed, because they are the bedrock, backbone of our economy.

We believe that our kids deserve good daycare and public schools. We believe our kids deserve public schools where students can learn and teachers can teach. And we wanna believe that our parents will have a good retirement and that we will too. We Democrats believe that social security is a pact that can not be broken.

We wanna believe that we can live out our lives without the terrible fear that an illness is going to bankrupt us and our children. We Democrats believe that America can overcome any problem, including the dreaded disease called AIDS. We believe that America is still a country where there is more to life than just a constant struggle for money. And we believe that America must have leaders who show us that our struggles amount to something and contribute to something larger—leaders who want us to be all that we can be.

We want leaders like Jesse Jackson. Jesse Jackson is a leader and a teacher who can open our hearts and open our minds and stir our very souls. And he has taught us that we are as good as our capacity for caring, caring about the drug problem, caring about crime, caring about education, and caring about each other.

Now, in contrast, the greatest nation of the free world has had a leader for eight straight years that has pretended that he can not hear our questions over the noise of the helicopters. And we know he doesn't wanna answer. But we have a lot of questions. And when we get our questions asked, or there is a leak, or an investigation the only answer we get is, "I don't know," or "I forgot."

But you wouldn't accept that answer from your children. I wouldn't. Don't tell me "you don't know" or "you forgot." We're not going to have the America that we want until we elect leaders who are gonna tell the truth; not most days but every day; leaders who don't forget what they don't want to remember. And for eight straight years George Bush hasn't displayed the slightest interest in anything we care about. And now that he's after a job that he can't get appointed to, he's like Columbus discovering America. He's found child care. He's found education. Poor George. He can't help it. He was born with a silver foot in his mouth.

Well, no wonder. No wonder we can't figure it out. Because the leadership of this nation is telling us one thing on TV and doing something entirely different. They tell us—They tell us that they're fighting a war against terrorists. And then we find out that the White House is selling arms to the Ayatollah. They—They tell us that they're fighting a war on drugs and then people come on TV and testify that the CIA and the DEA and the FBI knew they were flying drugs into America all along. And they're negotiating with a dictator who is shoveling cocaine into this country like crazy. I guess that's their Central American strategy.

Now they tell us that employment rates are great, and that they're for equal opportunity. But we know it takes two paychecks to make ends meet today, when it used to take one. And the opportunity they're so proud of is low-wage, dead-end jobs. And there is no major city in America where you cannot see homeless men sitting in parking lots holding signs that say, "I will work for food."

Now my friends, we really are at a crucial point in American history. Under this Administration we have devoted our resources into making this country a military colossus. But we've let our economic lines of defense fall into disrepair. The debt of this nation is greater than it has ever been in our history. We fought a world war on less debt than the Republicans have built up in the last eight years. You know, it's kind of like that brother-in-law who drives a flashy new car, but he's always borrowing money from you to make the payments.

Well, but let's take what they are most proudest of—that is their stand of defense. We Democrats are committed to a strong America, and, quite frankly, when our leaders say to us, "We need a new weapons system," our inclination is to say, "Well, they must be right." But when we pay billions for planes that won't fly, billions for tanks that won't fire, and billions for systems that won't work, "that old dog won't hunt." And you don't have to be from Waco to know that when the Pentagon makes crooks rich and doesn't make America strong, that it's a bum deal.

Now I'm going to tell you, I'm really glad that our young people missed the Depression and missed the great Big War. But I do regret that they missed the leaders that I knew, leaders who told us when things were tough, and that we'd have to sacrifice, and that these difficulties might last for a while. They didn't tell us things were hard for us because we were different, or isolated, or special interests. They brought us together and they gave us a sense of national purpose. They gave us Social Security and they told us they were setting up a system where we could pay our own money in, and when the time came for our retirement we could take the money out. People in the rural areas were told that we deserved to have electric lights, and they were gonna harness the energy that was necessary to give us electricity so my grandmamma didn't have to carry that old coal oil lamp around. And they told us that they were gonna guarant[ee] when we put our money in the bank, that the money was going to be there, and it was going to be insured. They did not lie to us.

And I think one of the saving graces of Democrats is that we are candid. We talk straight talk. We tell people what we think. And that tradition and those values live today in Michael Dukakis from Massachusetts.

Michael Dukakis knows that this country is on the edge of a great new era, that we're not afraid of change, that we're for thoughtful, truthful, strong leadership. Behind his calm there's an impatience to unify this country and to get on with the future. His instincts are deeply American. They're tough and they're generous. And personally, I have to tell you that I have never met a man who had a more remarkable sense about what is really important in life.

And then there's my friend and my teacher for many years, Senator Lloyd Bentsen. And I couldn't be prouder, both as a Texan and as a

Democrat, because Lloyd Bentsen understands America. From the barrio to the boardroom, he knows how to bring us together, by regions, by economics, and by example. And he's already beaten George Bush once.

So, when it comes right down to it, this election is a contest between those who are satisfied with what they have and those who know we can do better. That's what this election is really all about. It's about the American dream—those who want to keep it for the few and those who know it must be nurtured and passed along.

I'm a grandmother now. And I have one nearly perfect granddaughter named Lily. And when I hold that grandbaby, I feel the continuity of life that unites us, that binds generation to generation, that ties us with each other. And sometimes I spread that Baptist pallet out on the floor, and Lily and I roll a ball back and forth. And I think of all the families like mine, like the one in Lorena, Texas, like the ones that nurture children all across America. And as I look at Lily, I know that it is within families that we learn both the need to respect individual human dignity and to work together for our common good. Within our families, within our nation, it is the same.

And as I sit there, I wonder if she'll ever grasp the changes I've seen in my life—if she'll ever believe that there was a time when blacks could not drink from public water fountains, when Hispanic children were punished for speaking Spanish in the public schools, and women couldn't vote.

I think of all the political fights I've fought, and all the compromises I've had to accept as part payment. And I think of all the small victories that have added up to national triumphs and all the things that would never have happened and all the people who would've been left behind if we had not reasoned and fought and won those battles together. And I will tell Lily that those triumphs were Democratic Party triumphs.

I want so much to tell Lily how far we've come, you and I. And as the ball rolls back and forth, I want to tell her how very lucky she is that for all our difference, we are still the greatest nation on this good earth. And our strength lies in the men and women who go to work every day, who struggle to balance their family and their jobs, and who should never, ever be forgotten.

I just hope that like her grandparents and her great-grandparents before that Lily goes on to raise her kids with the promise that echoes in homes all across America: that we can do better, and that's what this election is all about.

Thank you very much.

Mary Fisher

(b. 1948)

A WHISPER OF AIDS
August 19, 1992

Mary Fisher is a nationally recognized artist and one of our country's most influential advocates for AIDS awareness. In 1992, Fisher founded the Family AIDS Network, which went on to become the Mary Fisher Center for AIDS Research and Education (CARE) Fund at the University of Alabama/Birmingham. The CARE Fund is a national non-profit organization that promotes AIDS awareness, while supporting clinical and outcomes-based research for persons suffering from HIV/AIDS. The following speech, delivered on August 19, 1992, at the Republican National Convention, launched Mary Fisher into the national spotlight, drawing much-needed attention to the issue of AIDS awareness in America.

LESS THAN three months ago at platform hearings in Salt Lake City, I asked the Republican Party to lift the shroud of silence which has been draped over the issue of HIV and AIDS. I have come tonight to bring our silence to an end. I bear a message of challenge, not self-congratulation. I want your attention, not your applause.

I would never have asked to be HIV positive, but I believe that in all things there is a purpose; and I stand before you and before the nation gladly. The reality of AIDS is brutally clear. Two hundred thousand Americans are dead or dying. A million more are infected. Worldwide, forty million, sixty million, or a hundred million infections will be counted in the coming few years. But despite science and research, White House meetings, and congressional hearings, despite good intentions and bold initiatives, campaign slogans, and hopeful promises, it is—despite it all—the epidemic which is winning tonight.

In the context of an election year, I ask you, here in this great hall, or listening in the quiet of your home, to recognize that AIDS virus is not a political creature. It does not care whether you are Democrat or Republican; it does not ask whether you are black or white, male or female, gay or straight, young or old.

Tonight, I represent an AIDS community whose members have been reluctantly drafted from every segment of American society. Though I am white and a mother, I am one with a black infant struggling with tubes in a Philadelphia hospital. Though I am female and contracted this disease in marriage and enjoy the warm support of my family, I am one with the lonely gay man sheltering a flickering candle from the cold wind of his family's rejection.

This is not a distant threat. It is a present danger. The rate of infection is increasing fastest among women and children. Largely unknown a decade ago, AIDS is the third leading killer of young adult Americans today. But it won't be third for long, because unlike other diseases, this one travels. Adolescents don't give each other cancer or heart disease because they believe they are in love, but HIV is different; and we have helped it along. We have killed each other with our ignorance, our prejudice, and our silence.

We may take refuge in our stereotypes, but we cannot hide there long, because HIV asks only one thing of those it attacks. Are you human? And this is the right question. Are you human? Because people with HIV have not entered some alien state of being. They are human. They have not earned cruelty, and they do not deserve meanness. They don't benefit from being isolated or treated as outcasts. Each of them is exactly what God made: a person; not evil, deserving of our judgment; not victims, longing for our pity—people, ready for support and worthy of compassion.

My call to you, my Party, is to take a public stand, no less compassionate than that of the President and Mrs. Bush. They have embraced me and my family in memorable ways. In the place of judgment, they have shown affection. In difficult moments, they have raised our spirits. In the darkest hours, I have seen them reaching not only to me, but also to my parents, armed with that stunning grief and special grace that comes only to parents who have themselves leaned too long over the bedside of a dying child.

With the President's leadership, much good has been done. Much of the good has gone unheralded, and as the President has insisted, much remains to be done. But we do the President's cause no good if we praise the American family but ignore a virus that destroys it.

We must be consistent if we are to be believed. We cannot love justice and ignore prejudice, love our children and fear to teach them. Whatever our role as parent or policymaker, we must act as eloquently as we speak—else we have no integrity. My call to the nation is a plea for awareness. If you believe you are safe, you are in danger. Because I was not hemophiliac, I was not at risk. Because I was not gay, I was not at risk. Because I did not inject drugs, I was not at risk.

My father has devoted much of his lifetime guarding against another holocaust. He is part of the generation who heard Pastor Nemoellor come out of the Nazi death camps to say,

> "They came after the Jews, and I was not a Jew, so, I did not protest. They came after the trade unionists, and I was not a trade unionist, so, I did not protest. Then they came after the Roman Catholics, and I was not a Roman Catholic, so, I did not protest. Then they came after me, and there was no one left to protest."

The—The lesson history teaches is this: If you believe you are safe, you are at risk. If you do not see this killer stalking your children, look again. There is no family or community, no race or religion, no place left in America that is safe. Until we genuinely embrace this message, we are a nation at risk.

Tonight, HIV marches resolutely toward AIDS in more than a million American homes, littering its pathway with the bodies of the young—young men, young women, young parents, and young children. One of the families is mine. If it is true that HIV inevitably turns to AIDS, then my children will inevitably turn to orphans. My family has been a rock of support.

My 84-year-old father, who has pursued the healing of the nations, will not accept the premise that he cannot heal his daughter. My mother refuses to be broken. She still calls at midnight to tell wonderful jokes that make me laugh. Sisters and friends, and my brother Phillip, whose birthday is today, all have helped carry me over the hardest places. I am blessed, richly and deeply blessed, to have such a family.

But not all of you—But not all of you have been so blessed. You are HIV positive, but dare not say it. You have lost loved ones, but you dare not whisper the word AIDS. You weep silently. You grieve alone. I have a message for you. It is not you who should feel shame. It is we—we who tolerate ignorance and practice prejudice, we who have taught you to fear. We must lift our shroud of silence, making it safe for you to reach out for compassion. It is our task to seek safety for our children, not in quiet denial, but in effective action.

Someday our children will be grown. My son Max, now four, will take the measure of his mother. My son Zachary, now two, will sort through his memories. I may not be here to hear their judgments, but I know already what I hope they are. I want my children to know that their mother was not a victim. She was a messenger. I do not want them to think, as I once did, that courage is the absence of fear. I want them to know that courage is the strength to act wisely when most we are afraid. I want them to have the courage to step forward when called by their nation or their Party and give leadership, no matter what the personal cost.

I ask no more of you than I ask of myself or of my children. To the millions of you who are grieving, who are frightened, who have suffered the ravages of AIDS firsthand: Have courage, and you will find support. To the millions who are strong, I issue the plea: Set aside prejudice and politics to make room for compassion and sound policy.

To my children, I make this pledge: I will not give in, Zachary, because I draw my courage from you. Your silly giggle gives me hope; your gentle prayers give me strength; and you, my child, give me the reason to say to America, "You are at risk." And I will not rest, Max, until I have done all I can to make your world safe. I will seek a place where intimacy is not the prelude to suffering. I will not hurry to leave you, my children, but when I go, I pray that you will not suffer shame on my account.

To all within the sound of my voice, I appeal: Learn with me the lessons of history and of grace, so my children will not be afraid to say the word "AIDS" when I am gone. Then, their children and yours may not need to whisper it at all.

God bless the children, and God bless us all.

Good night.

Gloria Steinem

(b. 1934)

A 21ST CENTURY FEMINISM
February 13, 2002

Gloria Steinem is a journalist and women's rights leader, in addition to being a co-founder of both New York magazine and Ms. magazine, where she still serves as a contributing editor today. Steinem gained national attention as an outspoken advocate for women's rights throughout the 1960s, and in 1971 joined Bella Abzug, Shirley Chisholm, and Betty Friedan to form the National Women's Political Caucus. In the following speech, delivered at the Commonwealth Club on February 13, 2002, Steinem outlines her ideas of feminism in the post-9/11 world.

A GREAT DEAL of effort has gone into trying to make feminism misunderstood. Rush Limbaugh, of course, is chief among the culprits here, since he has coined the word "feminazi," which is especially offensive because it is ahistorical. The Nazis were anti-feminist and came to power specifically against feminism. But there have been other, more subtle efforts, just as there have been to demonize words like "liberal" and "affirmative action." Feminism means what it says in the dictionary: The belief in the whole social, political and economic equality of women and men. Obviously, women and men can and should be feminists.

It means a major revolution and transformation. It isn't the way the world is running. We are not looking at the world as if female human beings and people of all colors mattered, which is the goal of feminism. There is resistance to taking away the world's single biggest source of unpaid or underpaid labor, not to mention the world's means of reproduction, which is probably the reason why reproductive issues are the key to women's movements around the world—whether it is fighting against female genital mutilation in many countries of Africa and the Middle East, or smuggling contraception into Ireland, or the fight to be able to have children in safety as well as not to have children.

There are also other wonderful words. We don't have to say "feminism." We could say "women's liberation." We could say "womanist." We could say "mujerista." These are all good words that simply mean the full humanity of both women and men.

The patriarchal-nationalist system has been going on in various stages between five and eight thousand years. That's only 5 percent of human history, so maybe we should declare this an experiment that failed. Even in this young country there have been two waves. First was the suffragist and abolitionist wave, which took more than 100 years to gain for women of all races and men of color an identity as human beings. It's useful to remember how recently most of the people in this country would have been literally property, like tables and chairs. It's perhaps not surprising that it's going to take us another century to gain legal and social equality. The first stage of resistance to change has passed—that feminism isn't necessary, that a woman's position is natural, that "my wife or employee isn't interested in this feminism stuff." But the second stage is with us, which is that it used to be necessary, but it isn't anymore. There is always an article somewhere saying that the movement is over, when in fact it has just begun.

We have moved forward in this first stage in huge leaps of consciousness. We've made great incursions into the professions and in giving greater value to the all-female professions, but we are moving a barrier.

The barrier I experienced as a student was that "We don't hire women," or that if you married you lost pretty much all of your civil rights: your name, your credit rating, your legal domicile. That's gone. But it's still true that when you have been in a job for 10 or 15 years, you hit the glass ceiling, or you hit the sticky floor of the pink-colored ghetto, which is still where most women are. Yes, you can make an equal marriage now and not lose your civil rights. But when the first child is born, it becomes unequal again because, to put it mildly, men in general—though there are exceptions—do not care for infants and little children as much as women do. Until there is equality in the home, there won't be equality outside the home.

As long as women have two jobs, one inside the home and one outside, there can't be equality outside. The struggles are in a different place but still very much present. If any young woman is still asking herself if she can combine a career and family, that's a symbol of the kind of change we need, because probably many fewer young men are worrying to the same degree about how they can combine career and family. We don't have the structural changes in the system that we need so that all parents of small children can have a shorter work day, a shorter work week and can adjust their schedules to parenthood. We're the only industrialized democracy in the world without some national system of childcare, without some national system of health care, which women need 30 percent more than men do because of childbearing.

Some of the symbols and signals of the 21st century are with us in the stories of our individual lives. I get to hear a lot of them, because I'm instantly recognizable as a symbol of this change. Young women of my generation said, "I'm not going to be anything like my mother," which was a way of denying that we could and might well have the same fate, because if we could blame her we didn't have to admit that it could happen to us unless we changed the structure. But instead, young women now sometimes say to me that they hope they can have as interesting a life as their mothers. They come up to me after talks or in book lines and say, "This is my mom. She's my best friend. I so admire what she's done. I see how hard her life has been."

There are ways in which our expectations and, to some extent, our realities have changed. V–Day is a great symbol of 21st century feminism. It has turned into an event on over 1000 campuses every year, in more than 81 countries. It's raised over $30 million to efforts against violence against women, starting out the way all social justice movements start out: by telling the truth about our own lives.

Eve Ensler interviewed women about their own bodies; inviting them to talk about their own sexual and physical selves yielded these immensely diverse, entertaining, tragic, amazing monologues that include everything from early date experiences in Queens to rape camps in Bosnia. Because she recorded women's real words and told the truth and reenacted them and did it as if everyone mattered, it has continued and grown from a theater the size of a teacup in downtown Manhattan to Madison Square Garden. Initially, *The New York Times* would not publish the word "vagina" and Ensler could not publicize the play; even book publishers wouldn't put the word on the cover— which is why I ended up writing the introduction. It's the kind of event where you're not quite the same kind of person when you leave as when you arrived. That's symbolic to me both of where we are at the beginning of 21st century feminism and how far we have to go. We are still standing on the bank of the river, rescuing people who are drowning. We have not gone to the head of the river to keep them from falling in. That is the 21st century task.

We know what the causes of violence are and how deeply they are rooted in gender roles. The normalization of object-subject, conquered-conqueror, winner-loser, by gender roles convince the male half of the population—especially men of an upper class or so-called superior racial groups—that their sense of identity and masculinity depend on control and even dominance and violence. That is the root cause. But I don't see it much commented on that serial killers and senseless killers—people who go into some public space and kill people they don't know, not for robbery or any reason except to kill people—are all male, white and not poor. They have been raised to believe that they have a right to be in control. When that is flouted with other elements, other things come into play and murderers are produced.

As we read our newspapers, we discover who the hijackers and suicide bombers were on September 11 and indeed who the leadership of al Qaeda was: They are not poor. They are all male. They are from the groups in their own countries who have been led to expect a certain amount of control. It's quite amazing that they are not women, not poor, not the most despised racial groups in their own settings. Yet, do we see this remarked upon? No. I'm not trying to do a single-factor analysis of violence; there are many different factors. But this is the least remarked upon, and yet it is the most obvious.

The television commentators, after a senseless killing, ask what's wrong with our children. It is not our children. It is a very particular subset of our children. How can we humanize the gender roles so that young men are raised to understand that they have all human qualities? We've had the courage to raise our daughters more like our sons, but fewer of us have had the courage to raise our sons more like our daughters. Those so-called feminine qualities are only the qualities you need to raise children: empathy, patience, flexibility, compassion. They're present in every man just as they are in every woman.

If we were to examine the implications of these clear things that we need to do in the future, it would mean that we are overthrowing or humanizing five to eight thousand years of patriarchy, racism and nationalism. We weren't always organized by nationalism, and we don't have to be. We need to consider monotheism, too, because when God looks like the ruling class, we're all in trouble. It's a big job. But if we look back and see how far we've come, just in our lifetimes, and project that onto the future, we can understand just how much further we can see ourselves go. We lose heart sometimes, but if you ever get discouraged and feel disempowered—and certainly the minority forces that are still in control in much of our lives try to make us feel disempowered—just remember that even the toughest-minded physicist now admits that the flap of a butterfly's wing here can change the weather hundreds of miles away.

Jane Fonda

(b. 1937)

THE NEW FEMINISM
September 2004

Jane Fonda is one of the most well-known members of her generation, renowned as a political activist, writer, Academy Award-winning actress, fitness guru, model, and women's rights leader. Having first gained recognition as the talented daughter of the great actor Henry Fonda, Jane Fonda appeared in numerous television programs and motion pictures throughout the 1960s, using her celebrity to advocate for social justice and an end to the Vietnam War. Fonda still enjoys a successful career as a motion picture actress, while remaining an outspoken figure in to-day's political landscape. The following speech was delivered at the 3rd Annual Women and Power Conference, organized by Omega Institute and V-Day in September 2004.

THIS HAS BEEN an emotional three days. I don't think I'm the only one that has been filled with tears. They are tears of joy. When our bodies become tuning forks, vibrating with words spoken by sisters that enter us and hum with truth. Tears of realization not only that we are not alone, but that we are one.

Tears of recognition that all of us are on a journey and none of us have arrived at a destination. It's not just me. It's all of us.

Tears of relief to know that the path isn't supposed to be straight or easy or even. It's not just me that stumbles against obstacles. Gloria still does. Marion still does. And even Sister Chittister does. When my daughter read the brochure for this conference, she said, 'Oh, mom, its it's [sic] so New Age. Yoga, meditation. Inner peace. I thought it was going to be political. The elections are two months away.' Well, I understand her reaction. I would have had that reaction when I was 35. Or 45. Or 55.

Before I realized that if I was going to become an effective agent for change, I had some healing to do. And that things that we consider New Age, like music and dance and painting and drama therapy and prayer and laughter can be part of the healing process. I know that it was while I was laughing when I first saw Eve Ensler perform *The Vagina Monologues* that my feminism slipped out of my head and took up residence in my body. Where it has lived ever since ... Embodied at last.

Up until then I had been a feminist in the sense that I supported women. I brought gender issues into my movie roles. I helped women make their bodies strong. I read all the books. I thought I had it in my heart and my body. I didn't. I didn't. I didn't. It was too scary. It was like stepping off a cliff without knowing if there was a trampoline down below to catch me. It meant rearranging my cellular structure. It meant doing life differently. And I was too scared. Women have internalized patriarchy's tokens in various ways, but for me I silenced my true authentic voice all my life to keep a man. Because God forbid I should be without a man. Preferably an alpha male. Because without that, what would validate me.

And I needed to try to be perfect because I knew that if I wasn't perfect, I would never be loved. And as I sat on the panel yesterday, my sense of imperfection became focused on my body. I hated my body. It started around the beginning of adolescence. Before then I had been too busy climbing trees and wrestling with boys to worry about being perfect. What was more important than perfect was strong and brave. But then suddenly the wrestling became about sex and being popular and being right and good and perfect and fitting in. And then I became an actress in an imaged focused profession. And being competitive, I said, 'Well, damn. If I'm supposed to be perfect, I'll show them.' Which of course pitted me against other women and against myself. Because as Carl Jung said, perfection is for the Gods. Completeness is what we mortals must strive for. Perfection is the curse of patriarchy. It makes us hate ourselves. And you can't be embodied if you hate your body. So one of the things we have to do is help our girls to get angry. Angry. Not at their own bodies, but at the paradigm that does this to us, to all of us. Let us usher perfection to the door and learn that good enough is good enough.

There's a theory of behavioral change called social innoculation. Maybe some of you have daughters. Social innoculation. It means politicizing the problem. Let me tell you a story that explains this. In one of the ghettos of Chicago, young girls weren't going to school anymore. And community organizers weren't going to school anymore and they found out they didn't have the right Nike Jordan shoes. So the organizers did something differently. They invited all the boys going to school into the community center and they took a Nike Jordan shoe and they dissected it. They cut off one layer of the rubber and they said See this? This is not a God. This was made in Korea. People were paid slave wages to make this, robbing your mothers and fathers of jobs. And he cut off another slice. And so it went. Deconstructing the Nike Jordan sneaker so the boys would understand the false god that they had been worshipping. We need to name the problem so that our girls can say, 'It's not me and we're going to get mad.'

We also have to stop looking over our shoulder to see who is the expert with the plan. We're the experts. If we allow ourselves to listen to what Marion Woodman calls our feminine consciousness. But this has been muted in a lot of us by the power centered male belief center called patriarchy. I don't like that word. The first night Eve spoke about the old and new paradigm and never said the word. I guess I'm too canvenous. It's so rhetorical. It makes people's eyes glaze over. It did for me. The first time I ever heard Gloria Steinem use it back in the '70s, I thought, "Oh, my God, what that means is men are bad and we have to replace patriarchy with matriarchy." Of course, given the way women are different than men, maybe a dose of matriarchy wouldn't be bad, maybe balancing things out. My favorite ex-husband Ted Turner—maybe some of you saw him say it on Charlie Rose. Men, we had our chance and we blew it. We have to turn it over to women now.

But I've come to see that it's not about replacing one archy with another. It's about changing the social construct to one where power and its talisman, money, is not the chief operating principle. Now, governments—there's this dual journey that we're on. There's the inner journey, this New Age stuff which is critical and the outer journey. Let's talk about governments first. Governments normally work within the power paradigm and governments play a central role in making us who we are. An empathic government encourages a caring government. A greedy government leads to a greedy maybe. A government that operates from a might makes right place creates a nation of bullies. Envied perhaps by the rest of the world for its things, but hated for its lack of goodness.

I first noticed this phenomenon of government when—many years ago I was making a movie in a little town in Norway and there was a party scene. It was Ibsen's *Doll House*. It took three days to shoot and I had a lot of chance to spend time with the local people and I kept thinking there's something very different about these people.

It's—what can it be? There's no hard edges. And as I began to talk to them I realized it's because they felt seen by their government. They felt valued. They mattered. Pregnant women got free milk. There was maternity leave. All the things that make women's and men's lives easier was addressed by their government. The only time I saw this addressed is Michael Moore's *Bowling For Columbine*. He asks this very interesting question. The Canadians have the same T.V. shows and video games and more guns per capita, but they're not violent. Of course we don't lock our doors. Are you kidding? And then he interviews three or four teenagers in the parking lot of a fast food restaurant. They look just like ours, tattooed and pierced and every-thing like that. But they don't lock their doors. And they said to him, of course health care is our birthright. And of course we are taken care of. By our government. And that's the difference. He didn't spell it out explicitly, but that's the message.

I never told these stories in a context like this, but I'm going to tell you two stories.

I went to Hanoi in 1972 in July. And I was there while my govern-ment was bombing the country that had received me as a guest. And I was in a lot of air raids. And I was taken into a lot of air raid shelters. And I noticed that every time I would go into a shelter, including one which was in a hospital because I had a broken foot, so I was with patients in an air raid shelter during a bombing raid. And the Vietnamese people would look at me and ask the interpreter—prob-ably they thought I was Russian—who was this white woman. And when the interpreter would say American, they would get all excited and they would smile at me.

And I would search their eyes for anger. I wanted to see anger. It would have made it easier if I could have seen what I know what I would have in my eyes if I were them. But I never did. Ever. And one day I had been taken several hours south of Hanoi to visit what had been the textile capital of north Vietnam that was raised to the ground and we were in the car and suddenly the driver and my in-terpreter said, "Quick, get out!" All along the road there are these manholes that hold one person and you jump in them and you pull kind of a straw lid over to protect you from shrapnel if there's a raid. I couldn't even hear bombs coming because they weren't raid. I was running down the street to get into one of these holes and suddenly I was grabbed from behind by a young girl. She was clearly a school girl because she had a bunch of books tied with a rubber belt hanging over her shoulder and she grabbed me by the hand and ran with me in front of this peasant hut. And she pulled the straw thatch off the top of the hole and jumped in and pulled me in afterward. These are small holes. These are meant for one small Vietnamese person. She and I got in the hole and she pulled the lid over and the bombs started dropping and causing the ground to shake and I'm thinking, this is not happening. I'm going to wake up. I'm not in a bomb hole with a Vietnamese girl whom I don't know. I could feel her breath on my cheek. I could feel her eye lash on my cheek. It was so small that we were crammed together.

Pretty soon the bombing stopped. It turned out it was not that close. She crawled out and I got out and I started to cry and I just said to her, "I'm so sorry. I'm so sorry. I'm so sorry." And she started to talk to me in Vietnamese. And the translator came over.

She must have been 15, 14. And she looked me straight in the eye and she said, "Don't be sorry for us. We know why we're fighting. It's you who don't know ..."

Well, it couldn't have been staged. It was impossible for it to have been staged. And I thought this young girl who says to me it's you—you have to cry for your own people because we know why we're fighting. And I'm thinking this must be a country of saints or something. Nobody gets angry.

Several days later I'm asked to go see a production of a play—a traveling troop of Vietnamese actresses is performing. It's Arthur Miller's play, *You Are My Sons*. They want me as an American to critique it to say if the capitalists are really the way they look. Two toned saddle shoes and a polka dot tie and I was like, OK, that will work. It's a story about a factory owner who makes parts for bombers during the second world war. He finds out that his factory is making faulty parts for the bombers, which could cause an airplane crash, but he doesn't say anything because he doesn't want to lose his government contract. One of his sons is a pilot and dies in an airplane crash. The other son accuses a—attacks his father for putting greed and self-interest ahead of what was right. Well, I watched the play and I kept thinking why are they—why are they—there's a war going on. Why are they performing *All My Sons*, a Vietnamese traveling troop of actors in North Vietnam. And I asked the director, "Why are you doing this?" And he said, "We are a small country. We cannot afford to hate you. We have to teach our people there are good Americans and there are bad Americans. So that they will not hate Americans because one day when this war ends, we will have to be friends."

When you come back home from a thing like that and people talk about enemy, you think, "Wait a minute. Will we ever have a government here that will go to such sophisticated lengths to help our people not hate a country that is bombing them?" This is the kind of government—and I don't want to romanticize the Vietnamese—it has not turned out—although we spend billions of dollars in tourist money over there.

Anyway, this is what I mean by the role of a government. This wasn't an accident that people didn't look at me during a war with hatred in their eyes. Their government taught them to love and to separate good from evil. That to me is a lesson that I will never ever forget.

So there's a dual journey to be taken. There's an inner journey and an outer journey and there's no conceptual model for the vision that we're working for. There's no road map for the politics of love. It's never happened.

Women have never yet had a chance in all of history to make a revolution. But if we're going to lead, we have to become the change that we seek. We have to incubate it in our bodies and embody it. When you think about it all the most impactful teachers, healers, activists are always people who embody their politics. I'm going to tell you another story. I have been living in France for eight years from 1962 to 1970 and I decided to leave my—not my favorite ex-husband, but my first ex-husband and come home to be an activist. And I realized that in order to do that properly, I had to get to know this country of mine again. And I decided that I was going to drive across the country for two months. It was during the spring of 1970. And as I was driving, Nixon invaded Cambodia. Four students were killed at Kent State, two at Jackson State, 35,000 National Guard were called out in 16 states and a third of the nation's campuses closed down. I was arrested five times. But when I think back over those difficult two months, none of that is what I remember.

I remember a woman who was on the staff of a GI coffee house in Texas near Fort Hood. Her name was Terry Davis. And the moment I was in her presence, I sensed something different. It wasn't something I had been missing because I didn't know it existed. But I felt different in her presence. Because she moved from a place of love. She saw me not as a movie star, but as a whole me that I didn't even know existed yet.

She was interested in why I had become an activist and what I was doing to get involved in the movement and we were planning an upcoming demonstration and she asked my opinion. And she included me in all the decisions to make sure I was comfortable. This was—this was very new for me. I was 31 years old. I made *Barbarella*. I was famous. But this was new to me. I saw the same sensitivity and compassion in the way she dealt with the GIs from Fort Hood at the coffee house. Unlike others in the peace movement at that time she didn't judge the young men who were on their way to Vietnam. She knew most of them were from poor rural or inner city situations and had no good alternatives.

It was my first time experiencing a woman's leadership and it was palpable, like sinking into a warm tub after a cold winter. It was also my first time experiencing someone who embodied her politics, who tried to model in her every day life the sort of society that she was fighting for. She fought not only against the government that was waging the war and depriving soldiers of their basic rights, she also fought against the sexism, the power struggles and judgmentalism within the movement itself. During that difficult two month trip, it was this time spent with Terry that stands out most deeply. A harbinger of the new world beyond isms and archies that I could envision because of her. She was in her power.

I chaired the campaign for adolescent pregnancy prevention, so I can't talk about power without talking about choice. You know, I used to wonder how is it that the so called pro-lifers show so much concern for the fetus, the fertilized egg growing inside the woman, but so little concern for the woman herself. Or even for the child once it is born.

And then I realized it's because this whole issue has nothing to do with being pro-life or pro-fetus. It has everything to do with power and who has it.

Throughout history many of the most patriarchial regimes and institution—Hitler, Pinoche, the Vatican, Bush, have been the most opposed to women controlling their reproduction. The life of the fetus is only the most recent strategy. In other countries at other times it's been national security, upholding the national culture. There have been many strategies.

But we have to understand reproduction and sexuality are keys to women's empowerment. Child bearing and child rearing is a— they're complex undertakings that can't be decided by a medical doctor or by policy makers or aging bishops. Celibate on top of it.

Because that makes a woman an object. It dismisses her knowledge about her own body and her own life. And instead of enhancing her dignity and self-respect it belittles and disempowers her. Robbed of her reproductive health and contraceptive decision making, a woman loses an essential element of what it means to be human. We have to hold this reproductive choice as a basic human right.

I want to talk about men for a minute. Because it's important—one of the things as I've been through three marriages now and I'm writing my memoirs so I thought deeply about the marriages and my husbands and my father and I feel it has made me love them even more because I have come to realize that patriarchy is toxic to men as well as women. We don't see it so clearly because in some ways it privileges them and it's kind of—well, men will be men. That's the way things are ... But it's why men split off from their emotions. Why the empathy gene is plucked from their hearts. Why there's a bifurcation from between their head and their heart.

The system that undermines the notion of masculinity, what it means to be a real man, is a poison that runs deep and crosses generations. Fathers learn the steps to the non-relational dance of patriarchy at their father's knees and their fathers probably learned it at the grandfather's knees. So the toxins continue generation after generation until now. We have to change the steps of the dance for ourselves and for our children.

Gloria Steinem said in one of her books that we need to change patriarchal institutions if we are to stop producing leaders whose lives are then played out on a national and international stage.

About four years ago I got to know Carol Gilligan. She is a feminist psychologist who transformed the landscape of psychology. It was like, oh, yeah. Women are left out. We better put them in. It's just fascinating.

I just want to touch on it very briefly. What I learned, which helped me understand my own life a lot better and the lives of the girls that I work with, it's when girls reach puberty that the damage begins. Up until then we— you know, if you can remember, if you can think and remember how feisty before and owned your voice. And then this thing happened and we lose it. And of course teaching our girls to maintain resistance and not go underground with it is critical. And it's so important for mothers to own our power because, I mean, I've had a very difficult relationship with my daughter and I know why. I'm like her rehearsal. I'm the one that's showing her what it's going to be like. And what did she see? She saw me giving away my power. Marriage after marriage after relationship. And she's been pissed all her life.

So it happens to us at 12, 13, 14. But Carol Gilligan has three sons like Sally. So she cares about boys. And she's researched boys. And she and her colleagues—you know what they discovered? The damage is done to boys around age five when they enter formal schooling. One out of ten young boys age five and six are on Ritalin in this country. It's when they—it's not even so much the parents are saying anything specific to them. They're entering the world and the message is, don't be a sissy or a mama's boy. Forget your emotions. They become emotionally illiterate.

Understand what that means as activists. Of course girls are the agents of change. You don't have to scratch very deep for us to say that's damn right. Man, I remember when I was ten and it wasn't like that at all.

But for boys, it's always been that way. They can't remember a time when they weren't entitled, when they weren't supposed to be this way, you know. They're at a tremendous disadvantage. And we have to hold that in our hearts and especially those of us that have young sons or in my case grandson—my grandson is five and he just entered kindergarten and you don't think I'm vigilant? They need— they need this combination of complete unconditional love and a lot of structure. But they have to be witnessed. They have to be seen. Some adult has to be present for them. And talking about the heart and about emotions to allow our young boys to come up and be worthy of our daughters.

So I want to say something about patriarchy and nature. I was on the board of the Turner Foundation. It was too hard, but my heart is still there because—I don't know. I mean nature is us. Get this book. Barbara Kennedy just wrote this book called the "War Against Nature". And it talks about how the Bush administration is the worst administration in terms of our environment. Every agency—every agency that is supposed to protect our environment is now headed by someone who runs a polluting industry. And it was on NPR the other day and he told the story. In the Tongass National Forest, there were trees alive when Christ walked the earth. There are five, six, seven hundred year-old cypress and cedar that have been valued at $20,000 on the stump that are being sold to the Alaska Pulp and Paper Company for $1.89. This is 100 percent Japanese owned. The trees are cut down and with the bark still on them they're shipped to Osaka Bay in Japan and they are stacked three stories deep underwater. Bobby Kennedy saw them because the Alaska Pulp and Paper Company gave a million dollars to the Bush administration.

I mean this is our irreplaceable national treasure. This is what our children will be able to—should be able to witness and revere in nature. And it's going, going, gone to some company that gave money to Bush. So that's another thing that we have to fight against.

I'm fascinated by this link between control of nature and control of women. It's very old, you know. Back in the 15th, 16th century, 9 million women were put on a rack or burned because they were different. At that same time Francis Bacon, who is called the father of reason—he's the one who came up with knowledge is power—that was his line—and he said we must put nature on the rack. Interesting. They were doing it to women and they said we have to do it to nature. And I'm on a spiritual quest, and so when I began to read the

Agnostic Gospels, specifically the ones found in 1945 in the deserts of Egypt, in one of them there's a new version of the Garden of Eden myth and it was an epiphany for me. And I understood why in the fourth century bishops had to say this is going to the Bible and this isn't. These books will not go in the Bible and they're going to be destroyed. Only some very brave monks put them in urns and vases and they've now been translated. Of course one of the things they say is God is in all of us. That's very radical because it means you don't need hierarchy; right? You don't need bishops. We contain it within ourselves. But then listen to this version of the Garden of Eden. I felt like someone had said welcome home.

God looks down—God looks down and sees Adam, man. And he says something is missing. All atoms and molecules are there and everything, but there's no consciousness. And so he sends down Eve, life, consciousness. The feminine spirit, light. She is dropped down and quickens the body of Adam into what today is our unique species. We are the only species who can observe the universe. We can be observers. I always wondered how come. Why? It's the feminine spirit. We didn't cause the downfall of man. We weren't an after thought. We quickened him into being. This incredible species that can observe God's creations.

That was when I really understood what Marion keeps talking about when she talks about the feminine consciousness. And robbing us of this by saying Eve caused the downfall, it has cut us off from our life source, from our Eve. God intended for there to be a balance.

That's why there's no archy. A balance between man, strength, balance, assertiveness—very important things to have. And a woman, fluid in the present, connected to earth, intuitive, chaotic. Every human being has both of those. We live in a matrix that combines those elements. And the danger is when it gets out of kilter. And where the masculine rises to the detriment of the feminine in an individual, in a nation, or in the world. What happens, then, war, lust, power, denigration of what's sacred.

So our task is to bring back the balance. In ourselves, in our families, our communities, and in the world.

It's so hard because patriarchy has been around so long that we just think that's life. It's ordained. An argument can be made that there was a time in history when it was necessary to build civilizations out of societies that were hunter gatherers. Somebody has to be in charge.

But you can also make an argument that that paradigm has—it's not only outlived its usefulness. It's become—it's destroying everything. It's destroying balance. It's destroying nature. It's destroying men. It's destroying women. So our task is to bring back balance. Our task is to elect the least patriarchal guy.

I vote for the one that says that terrorism has to be dealt with with sensitivity myself. And you know why? Because it's true.

All the experts on terrorism say you have to understand why young men want to blow themselves up. What is the cause of it? Before the conference started we were talking about this issue and John Kerry has been made fun of by Cheney because he said we have to be sensitive. But he said you know, supposing we had a president that would actually get a hold of Osama and said, "Let's talk." Remember the example she used about Gorbachev and Reagan. And for those of you who weren't here the first night—there was suddenly this thing happened where the arms race was turned around, was stopped. And someone asked Gorbachev what happened between you and Reagan. And he said we talked. Talking. There's a chemical change that happens when people really show up for each other. Imagine what would happen if we just sat down with Osama and said, 'OK. Now, tell me what's the problem?' And we really—it would be totally disarming, you know. It would be great.

You have to see a movie called *What the Bleep Do I Know*. It's playing to theaters in New York City. It's a tiny independent company out of Portland putting this out. It's about quantum physics, Judeo-Christian theories and change. One of the theories is, it's an experiment done by a Japanese scientist. It's true. The character in the movie played by Marlee Matlin, the wonderful deaf actress, she's in a subway and sees these huge vials of water and with photographs—with photographs over them. The first one explains the vial of water was taken from a large body of water in Japan and the cells were photographed through a microscope, just random. And they look very random. The second photograph was taken of the water cells when they had been blessed by a Buddhist monk. They were like snow flakes. They had reformed themselves into these beautiful structures because they had been blessed. And then there was another photograph of the cells where overnight the words "I love you" had been taped to the water and again, they were beautiful. They had changed again into these wonderful shapes. And then there was another one where the words had been taped "I hate you. I want to kill you." And the cells looked like knives. They were jagged and they were ugly and they were dangerous. And this man comes—this is true. This man comes up to her and says, it makes you think, doesn't it? You know, if a thought can do that to the cells of water, think what it can do to you.

And there's another story that's told—I didn't know anything about this. In 1993 in Washington D.C, 4,000 people came from all over the world to meditate. And they met with the police department in D.C. and they said we're going to meditate and the violent crime rate is going to drop. The police chief said, are you crazy? In Washington in the summertime? It would take two feet of snow to reduce the crime rate. Well, it did. 4,000 people from all over the world meditated for a week. And the violent crime rate dropped 25 percent. And the police were blown away. Totally blown away.

What this says is change is so mysterious and we must not lose hope. Embodiment, intentionality can make the difference if there's enough of us. That's why this conference is so important. If we can communicate through our hearts and souls and bodies what has happened to us today, that cellular change that has taken place—do you feel it? Yeah. If you can transfer that to the people you're going back to, we're going to become a tipping point. You know, what we're seeing now is the balance so out of kilter, so barnacled with the wrong kind of power and lust. But think about what happens to a wounded beast. It's always right before the beast dies that it becomes the most dangerous. And it thrashes and flails. But most of us who have been here today know that right beneath the surface, a great tactonic shift is taking place.

I'll tell you why I know it. Have you ever been to Yellowstone National Park? My cousin has. Yellowstone is the place in the world next to Siberia where the earth's crust is the most thin. Where the molten interior of the earth pops out. Old Faithful is the most well known example of this. But if you walk through the park you can see steam rising above the trees and over here mud bubbling up from cracks and crevices in the crust. I've travelled all over the world. Sometimes with Eve. Sometimes on my own. But I've seen the steam. And I've seen the mud bubbling up. And it's women and men all over the world that are starting to come through those cracks and crevices. It's an army of love and that's what we have to be. We have to ripen the time and turn that steam and those bubbles into a volcano. So let's be a volcano. Thank you. Thank you very much.

We're going to end this in prayer. We want to go out on a prayerful note.

Hillary Rodham Clinton

(b. 1947)

REMARKS ON THE REAUTHORIZATION
OF THE VOTING RIGHTS ACT

July 20, 2006

Hillary Rodham Clinton has had a long and esteemed career, including twelve years as the First Lady of Arkansas and eight years as the First Lady of the United States. Presently, she is the junior U.S. Senator from New York. Throughout her political life, Clinton has been a steadfast advocate for universal health care, women's rights, and education. The following address, delivered on the Senate floor on July 20, 2006, promotes the need for Congress to reauthorize the Voting Rights Act of 1965.

MR. PRESIDENT, I am also here to voice my support for the Fannie Lou Hamer, Rosa Parks, and Coretta Scott King Voting Rights Act Reauthorization and Amendments Act of 2006. It is so fitting that this legislation reauthorizing this landmark civil rights act would be named for three women who are so well known as heroines of the struggle for civil rights in our own country. Thousands of Americans risked their lives and some unfortunately lost them during the civil rights movement to challenge an electoral system that prevented millions of our fellow citizens from exercising their constitutional right to vote. After a long struggle by activists and everyday citizens, President Johnson introduced and eventually signed the Voting Rights Act of 1965 into law.

I vividly remember the day 41 years ago when I sat in front of our little black and white television set and watched President Johnson announce the signing into law of the Voting Rights Act.

He opened his speech to the nation that night with these memorable words: "I speak tonight for the dignity of man and the destiny of democracy." That was the culmination of a long struggle which continues even now, because we still must work vigilantly to make certain that those who try to vote are allowed to do so and that we keep watch to guarantee that every vote is counted.

President Johnson was right all those years ago. When you deny a person his or her right to vote, you strip that individual of dignity and you weaken our democracy.

The endurance of our democracy requires constant vigilance—a lesson that has been reinforced by the last two presidential elections, both of which were affected by widespread allegations of voter disenfranchisement.

Mr. President, I believe we have a moral as well as a political and historical obligation to ensure the integrity of our voting process. That was our nation's obligation in 1965. It remains our obligation today.

As we turn on our news and see the sights of conflict, as we hear the stories of sectarian violence, as we struggle to help nations understand and adopt democracy in their own lands, we more than ever must ensure that America is the place where the right to vote is fully and equally available to every citizen.

Now, we still have work to do to renew protections for the right to vote, to enforce safeguards that guarantee the right to vote, and strengthen our election laws so that our right to vote is not impeded by accident or abuse.

While parts of the Voting Rights Act are permanent, there are three important sections set to expire next year unless they are renewed. Section 5 of the Voting Rights Act requires that the federal government or a federal court approve, or in the language of the act, preclear, all changes to voting procedures by jurisdictions that have a history of discrimination.

Now, the importance of this provision cannot be overstated. Section 5 is the bulwark. It stands to ensure that all minorities have equal access to the ballot box. Not only has Section 5 been used to strike down potentially discriminatory changes to election laws, but it has also deterred them.

Equally important is the reauthorization of Sections 6 through 9 which authorize the federal government to send examiners and observers to jurisdictions with a history of voter discrimination and voter intimidation and to ensure that by the presence of the federal government, which represents all of us, that no one will engage in such despicable behavior.

Finally, Section 203 of the Voting Rights Act requires bilingual assistance for areas with a concentration of citizens with limited English proficiency, including bilingual ballots, if necessary. Voters with limited English proficiency would in many instances be unable to participate in our political process and to fully exercise their rights of citizenship if this assistance were not available to help them understand what's on a ballot. Sometimes even though I speak English, I think I need help understanding what's on some of our ballots when we have all kinds of bond issues and other kinds of activity. So imagine if you are, as some of the people whom I have met, an immigrant, a legal immigrant from Latin America who is so proud to be a citizen and so worried she'll make a mistake when she first goes to vote. An elderly gentleman who came to this country fleeing oppression in the former Soviet Union who speaks only Russian but has become a citizen, is learning English and wants to be able to understand what he is voting for.

At a time when we are embroiled in a debate about how best to assimilate immigrants and to send out the message that we want people in our country to learn English, to participate as citizens, we don't want to set up any artificial barriers to them feeling totally involved in and supportive of and welcomed by our great democracy.

These expiring sections of the Voting Rights Act, Sections 5, 203, 6 through 9, have all been reauthorized—first in the House, then in the Judiciary Committee yesterday here in the Senate. And I'm very pleased that that has happened because I think we still need them.

Of course, we've made so much progress. I'm very proud of the progress our nation has made. When you go back and look over more than 200 years of history, what have we accomplished, it's just a miraculous, wonderful happening that could only occur in this great country of ours where we have steadily and surely knocked down the barriers to participation. But are we perfect? Of course not. There is no such thing as perfection on this earth. And we have survived as a nation and as the oldest democracy in part because we've had checks and balances and we've been under the rule of law, not of men. And so this reauthorization is critical to making sure we still have the framework to make it possible for every person to feel that he or she can vote and that vote will matter.

Now, of course, the Voting Rights Act only works if it is actually enforced. You can have all the laws in the world. We've seen that in so many authoritarian regimes, totalitarian ones where they've got great founding laws. Laws like it's, you know, next to paradise but it doesn't matter because nobody enforces them. Well, unfortunately, I'm worried that we may be at that point in our own country when it comes to voting rights. The Civil Rights Division at the Department of Justice has been purged by many of the people who were career lawyers, who enforced the law regardless of whether it was against democrats or republicans or in any part of the country. Now it is filled with political appointees who often choose ideology over evidence, and I think that has resulted in a failure to enforce the Voting Rights Act.

There are lots of examples. You know, you can look at the news coverage this past December. Six career lawyers and two analysts in the Department of Justice's Civil Rights Division, it was reported, were basically overruled when they made recommendations about the Texas redistricting plan. The Civil Rights Division officials were overruled when they recommended against Georgia's voter photo ID requirement which disadvantaged African-Americans, the elderly and other voters. Finally that law was enjoined by a federal court.

These are isolated incidences in some people's minds but I see unfortunately a pattern here. We need to make sure our laws have teeth. Otherwise they're just for show and they don't make any difference at all.

Unfortunately, almost two-thirds of lawyers in the voting section of the Civil Rights Division have left in the last few years. And that sends a very disconcerting message that maybe, you know, the Voting Rights Act is going to be honored by word but not by deed.

So I hope that when we reauthorize it as I'm confident we will do here in the Senate, we will send a message that we expect it to be enforced and that it means something. Otherwise we're not going to be fulfilling the promise of a Constitution that sets voting and democracy at its core.

So I hope that we will not only reauthorize the Voting Rights Act—that we will enforce the Voting Rights Act, and that thirdly we will change some of our other laws to protect against some of the abuses that are now taking place around the country when it comes to voting. We have to strengthen our electoral system so that basic democratic values are protected as voting technology evolves and as it threatens to undermine the right to vote.

I think we need to put a few simple principles into law. We should do it sooner instead of later so that we count every vote and we make sure every vote is counted. That's why I drafted and introduced along with some of my colleagues in both houses the Count Every Vote Act because I believe that all Americans ought to have a reasonable opportunity to register and cast their vote if they are citizens. That should be just part of being a citizen.

In fact, I just met with a group of young high school students from New York and we were talking about how we could get more young people involved in voting. One of them said, well, when we turn 18 why aren't we automatically registered? I said that's a great idea. You should be automatically registered. We need to make this part of the growing up in America. You turn 18, you get registered to vote and you should start a lifetime habit of voting.

We also need to make sure that every American citizen will be able to count on the fact that their name will not be illegally purged from the voter rolls. We've seen that happen. It is still happening. It really bothers me because what happens is they, you know, somebody in the political position of a state says, well, let's purge the voter rolls because we want to get rid of people who have moved or who may not be eligible to vote. Well, I don't disagree with that. People who don't live in a jurisdiction or are not eligible shouldn't be permitted to vote. But instead of purging on that very limited basis often times they purge hundreds and thousands of people unfairly, unlawfully. And then someone shows up to vote and they are told, well, we're sorry, you are not registered to vote. The person doesn't know what has happened but then they are prohibited from voting.

Every American voter who shows up at the polls should be confident they don't have to wait hours to cast ballots. I did a town hall meeting in Cleveland with my friend Congresswoman Jones and we had testimony from people, including students from Kenyon College who had to wait between 10 and 12 hours to be able to vote. They were eligible. They were registered. They were anxious to vote. Because of the way the number of voting machines was allocated and the sort of discouragement that was meant to be sent that you would have to wait so long, it was a really unfair treatment of these young people and really not in keeping with our desire to increase the number of people who vote in our country.

We also need to make sure that the system of voting has not been compromised by politics or partisanship. I just think it's flat wrong for somebody who runs an election to also be running in the election and thereby be supervising their own election or for somebody to be running for election to some position, get the support of the position who is running the election as his campaign manager or spokesman. That's a conflict of interest that ought to be prohibited. People need to feel, and they have every right to feel confidence in the integrity of our electoral system.

And finally every American voter should know that there are adequate safeguards against abuses or mistakes caused by the new computerized voting machines. There have been so many problems. They've broken down. They have double counted. They have failed to count. Tests have been run showing how easy they are to hack into. You know, we don't need that. We need a system that people can count on. I mean, if we can go to an A.T.M. and withdraw money and if we can all have other kinds of advantages from the access to computers and the Internet and all the rest of it, for goodness sakes we ought to be able to use electronic voting without raising questions about whether it's been truthful and whether it's been accurate and whether it's even being operated correctly.

So, Mr. President, this effort to reauthorize the Voting Rights Act is part of a larger struggle about basic rights, basic values and basic opportunities. It is at root a struggle to ensure that we live up to the promise of democracy in this nation. So we do need to reinstate the decades old voting rights protections and we need to ensure those voting rights protections, and we need to strengthen those voting rights protections. We need to do that because that's who we are as Americans. That is what we expect of ourselves. And I hope that after we reauthorize the Voting Rights Act, which I'm confident we're going to do, that then we turn our attention to making sure we enforce it. And then we ask ourselves, are we doing everything we can to encourage people to vote and make it as easy for them to vote and make sure every vote counts.

Our ideals are important to us as Americans. Our principles about who we are, what we believe in are really core values as to what it means to be an American. And I only can hope and trust that when it comes to the most important function in a democracy, namely, running elections, and giving people the right to make decisions about who governs us, that we will be second to none. We cannot say that now because other countries, frankly, are doing a better job than we are but today is a good first step to get us back on the track of making sure that the world's oldest democracy demonstrates clearly we know how to run elections that people have confidence and trust in and that we want every single citizen to feel welcome to participate and to make the decisions that will determine the future of our country.

Nancy Pelosi

(b. 1940)

SPEECH UPON HER ELECTION
AS SPEAKER OF THE HOUSE
January 4, 2007

*Nancy Pelosi has represented the 8th Congressional District of California
since her election to the office in 1987. During her tenure as a congresswoman, Pelosi has been a powerful advocate for civil liberties, minority
rights, women's rights, and education. With her election as Speaker of
the House in 2006, Pelosi became the highest-ranking woman in the
history of the United States government. The following speech was delivered before the U.S. House of Representatives on January 4, 2007.*

THANK YOU MY COLLEAGUES, thank you leader (John) Boehner
(R-Ohio).

I accept this gavel in the spirit of partnership, not partisanship, and
I look forward to working with you Mr. Boehner and the Republicans
in the Congress on behalf of the American people.

After giving away this gavel in the last two Congress', I'm glad
someone else had the honor today.

In this House, we may belong to different parties, but we serve one
country. We stand united in our pride and prayers for our men and
women in the armed forces. They are working together to protect
America, and we, in this House, must also work together to build a
future worthy of their sacrifice.

In this hour, we need and pray for the character, courage, and civility of a former member of this House—President Ford. He healed
the country when it needed healing. This is another time, another
war, and another trial of our American will, imagination, and spirit.
Let us honor his memory, not just in eulogy, but in dialogue and trust
across the aisle. Let us express our condolences and appreciation to

Mrs. Ford and the entire Ford family for their decades of service to our country.

With today's convening of the 110th Congress, we begin anew. I congratulate all members of Congress on your election; I especially want to congratulate our new members of Congress. The genius of our Founders was that every two years, new members bring to this House their spirit of renewal and hope for the American people. This Congress is reinvigorated new members by your optimism, your idealism, and your commitment to our country. Let us acknowledge your families, whose support has made your leadership possible.

Each of us brings to this new Congress our shared values, our commitment to the Constitution, and our personal experience.

My path to Congress and the speakership began in Baltimore where my father was mayor. I was raised in a large family that was devoutly Catholic, deeply patriotic, very proud of our Italian American heritage, and staunchly Democratic. My parents taught us that public service was a noble calling, and that we had a responsibility to help those in need. I viewed them as working on the side of the angels and now they are with them.

I am so proud that my brother Tommy D'Alesandro, who was also a mayor of Baltimore, is here leading my D'Alesandro family today.

Forty-three years ago, Paul Pelosi and I were married. We raised our five children in San Francisco, where Paul was born and raised. I want to thank Paul and our children Nancy Corinne, Christine, Jacqueline, Paul, and Alexandra and our six magnificent grandchildren for giving me their love, support and the confidence to go from the kitchen to the Congress.

And I thank my constituents in San Francisco and to the state of California for the privilege of representing them in Congress. Saint Francis of Assisi is our city's patron saint, and his song of St. Francis is our city's anthem: 'Lord, make me a channel of thy peace; where there is darkness may we bring light, where there is hatred, may we bring love, and where there is despair, may we bring hope.'

Hope, hope, that is what America is about and it is in that spirit that I was sent to Congress.

And today, I thank my colleagues. By electing me speaker, you have brought us closer to the ideal of equality that is America's heritage and America's hope.

This is an historic moment—and I thank the leader for acknowledging it. I thank you Leader Boehner. It is an historic moment for the Congress, and an historic moment for the women of this country. It is a moment for which we have waited over 200 years. Never losing faith, we waited through the many years of struggle to achieve our rights. But women weren't just waiting; women were working. Never losing faith, we worked to redeem the promise of America, that all men and women are created equal. For our daughters and granddaughters, today we have broken the marble ceiling. For our daughters and our granddaughters, the sky is the limit, anything is possible for them.

The election of 2006 was a call to change—not merely to change the control of Congress, but for a new direction for our country. Nowhere were the American people more clear about the need for a new direction than in the war in Iraq.

The American people rejected an open-ended obligation to a war without end. Shortly, President Bush will address the nation on the subject of Iraq. It is the responsibility of the president to articulate a new plan for Iraq that makes it clear to the Iraqis that they must defend their own streets and their own security, a plan that promotes stability in the region, and a plan that allows us to responsibly redeploy our troops.

Let us work together to be the Congress that rebuilds our military to meet the national security challenges of the 21st century.

Let us be the Congress that strongly honors our responsibility to protect the American people from terrorism.

Let us be the Congress that never forgets our commitment to our veterans and our first responders, always honoring them as the heroes that they are.

The American people also spoke clearly for a new direction here at home—they desire a new vision, a new America, built on the values that have made our country great.

Our founders envisioned a new America driven by optimism, opportunity, and strength. So confident were they in the America they were advancing, they put on the seal, the great seal of the United States, 'novus ordo seclorum'—a new order for the centuries. Centuries, they spoke of the centuries. They envisioned America as a just and good place, as a fair and efficient society, as a source of opportunity for all.

This vision has sustained us for over 200 years, and it accounts for what is best in our great nation: liberty, opportunity, and justice.

Now it is our responsibility to carry forth that vision of a new America into the 21st Century.

A new America that seizes the future and forges 21st Century solutions through discovery, creativity, and innovation, sustaining our economic leadership and ensuring our national security.

A new America with a vibrant and strengthened middle class for whom college is affordable, health care is accessible, and retirement reliable.

A new America that declares our energy independence, promotes domestic sources of renewable energy, and combats climate change.

A new America that is strong, secure, and a respected leader among the community of nations.

And the American people told us they expected us to work together for fiscal responsibility, with the highest ethical standards and with civility and bipartisanship.

After years of historic deficits, this 110th Congress will commit itself to a higher standard: pay as you go, no new deficit spending. Our new America will provide unlimited opportunity for future generations, not burden them with mountains of debt.

In order to achieve our new America for the 21st Century, we must return this House to the American people. So our first order of business is passing the toughest congressional ethics reform in history. This new Congress doesn't have two years or 200 days.

Let us join together in the first 100 hours to make this Congress the most honest and open Congress in history—100 hours.

This openness requires respect for every voice in the Congress. As Thomas Jefferson said, 'Every difference of opinion is not a difference of principle.' My colleagues elected me to be Speaker of the House— the entire House. Respectful of the vision of our Founders, the expectations of our people, and the great challenges that we face, we have an obligation to reach beyond partisanship to work for all Americans.

Let us all stand together to move our country forward, seeking common ground for the common good.

We have made history, now let us make progress for our the America people.

May God bless our work, and may God bless America.